Blue and Gray Laughing

Blue and Gray Laughing

A Collection of
Civil War Soldiers' Humor

Edited by Paul Zall

Rank And File Publications
Redondo Beach, California
1996

Publisher's Cataloging in Publication

Zall, Paul M.
    Blue and gray laughing : a collection of Civil War soldier's
humor / Paul Zall.
    p. cm.
    ISBN 0-9638993-7-6

    1. United States--History--Civil War, 1861-1865--Humor.   I.
Title.

E655.Z35 1996   973.7'8

Table of Contents

Currier and Ives 1861

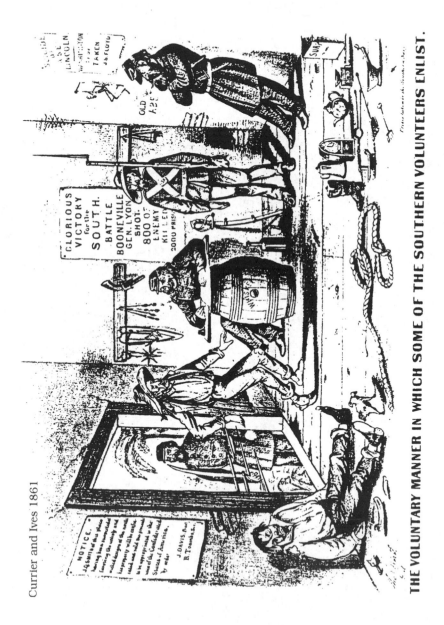

THE VOLUNTARY MANNER IN WHICH SOME OF THE SOUTHERN VOLUNTEERS ENLIST.

"Didja hear the one about. . . ?" How many soldiers in how many wars have opened the evening campfire discussion with that line?

Humorous graffiti has been found scratched by soldiers on the walls of ancient Pompeii. Bawdy and witty stories and songs have been part of the repertoire of fighting men throughout the ages; the boys in blue and gray did not shirk their responsibility and obligation to this tradition.

Someone once said, "Soldiers must laugh to keep from crying." This old saw must be true. While much tragedy and drama may be unearthed in soldiers' letters, a good deal of humor and irony will also be found. Civil War soldiers loved to make fun of authority, to complain about just damned near anything, and to toot their own horn whenever possible. Humor provided the vehicle they used to accomplish all these goals.

Soldiers told jokes and wrote down their humorous observations in letters, journals and diaries, and even sent them home to their local newspapers and periodicals. Many were no doubt too bawdy for polite publications. These contemporary sallies at wit, usually expressed in the form of "telling stories funny" rather than "telling funny stories," were often far more pungent and biting than the time-mellowed comments found in most memoirs.

Professor Paul Zall, author of several books on American humor including *Abe Lincoln Laughing, Mark Twain Laughing, Ben Franklin Laughing,* and several others, is currently Research Scholar at the Huntington Library. He thoroughly understands Civil War soldiers and their humor, and rightly suggests that you will get much more out of these stories if you read them aloud–as though *you* were the soldier-storyteller–complete with pregnant pauses to leave time for loud guffaws or even a few sniffs of disapproval and a loud groan or two at the "quality" of the wit. And please do read them enthusiastically, for you know that is how they were told, each man waiting his turn in a sort of Civil War "can you top this?" contest.

Making humor from human foibles and conditions is as old as mankind, and, to the soldier, no doubt as comforting as any activity he could do in public by himself. Some of these stories had no doubt been around for decades or even centuries, while others hung around to become staples of vaudeville and the *Joe Smith Joke Book* with all its spinoffs. Willie and Joe, World War II's "common soldiers," would recognize many of them.

Much has been written of the horror and tragedy of *our war*; it is refreshing to have this bit of laughter to lighten the shadows. Every Civil War speaker should be grateful to Dr. Zall for his wonderful gathering of wit and humor: many of these stories will find their way into the opening remarks of speakers at Civil War Round Tables and other organizations throughout the country. And the average Civil War buff will probably find this to be an excellent, lighthearted gift for a friend.

It is also fitting that through the generosity of Dr. Zall and Rank and File Publications, the proceeds of a book essentially "written" by Civil War soldiers should be used to preserve and commemorate the hallowed grounds where so many of those very soldiers fought and died. Those of us who study the Civil War have an obligation to save as many of the actual battlefields as is reasonable and practical. Dr. Zall's concern for battlefield preservation will help in this effort.

All in all, *Blue and Gray Laughing* is a welcome addition to Civil War literature. And a funny one. Civil War soldiers needed humor. In today's world, we probably need more books like this one.

Jerry Russell
National Chairman
Civil War Round Table Associates

Introduction:
Good Humor in Bad Times

A boy growing up in Lowell, Massachusetts in the early 1920s couldn't help listening to ancient veterans of the GAR swapping stories of what they had done in the War. It seemed strange that they could joke about the horrors they had seen, but now I realize they had used humor to hide the pain of memory – just as during the war they had used it to heal the hurt and solace the soul under stress.

It is too bad that their stories could not have been tape-recorded for posterity. As mere substitute, I have compiled printed versions, but these are hardly anything like the way the stories were performed–in an age when everything written down would have been read aloud. Readers who therefore depend on reading by eye rather than by ear may miss much of the humor unless they try reading aloud, with gusto.

My resources for the printed versions are the remarkable collections in the Henry E. Huntington Library, in San Marino, California. Here I have been able to mine diaries, journals, and correspondence of the soldiers themselves, and especially the contributions they made to newspapers and periodicals of the day instead of later memoirs colored by romantic haze. And I have also been able to concentrate on common soldiers rather than the professional writers usually reprinted as surrogates.

These citizen-soldiers wrote more than any warriors before them. Literacy rates on both sides surpassed 80 per cent. They had more newspapers per capita then than we have now. Telegraph and rail lines served wire services and made mass-circulating magazines available coast to coast. The troops published their own newspapers by means of portable presses or commandeered printing establishments, with 126 Federal and 15 Confederate publications surviving. African-American troops in Louisiana even published their own, *Black Warrior*.

Along with newspapers from home and the periodicals that crisscrossed enemy lines during prisoner exchanges and between pickets, their own newspapers gave the troops outlets for gripes, rumors, morale boosters, and

Harper's Monthly May 1861   ENLISTMENT OF SICKLES' BRIGADE, N. Y.

especially humor from field, camp or hospital. Some of these humorous stories open a window on the hearts and minds of soldiers on both sides, revealing what any student of human nature would expect to find: that those in blue and gray were more alike than different.

Lincoln appreciated that fact. Wit and humor of soldiers North or South were equally welcome to him, and he shared their laughter at the pretensions of those in authority, including himself. One of his favorites described Major General Foster escorting Secretary of War Edwin Stanton upriver at Port Royal when a picket shouted: "Who's aboard that tug?" "The Secretary of War and Major General Foster!" The picket roared back: "We've got enough major-generals up here–send some hardtack." The President valued any story that showed "the boys" using pleasantry and mirth to ease their privations. It seemed to him "as if neither death nor danger could quench" their grim humor. He would clip excerpts from the newspapers to memorize and utilize to hide his own pain, heal his own hurt, solace his own soul.

Some of their stories were old friends indeed, passing by word-of-mouth for centuries – as in the story of two soldiers returning to camp from a night on the town, meeting an old farm-wife and her cow: "Good morning, mother of asses!" "Good morning, my sons." Time, place, and circumstances may have changed, but the facetiae were familiar. In fact, frequently the same story appears in print on both sides of the frontlines, sometimes substituting, perhaps, General Sherman for General Stonewall Jackson, clearly the favorite humor-hero of the Confederates, with General Leonidas Polk a close second. Lincoln is their only close competitor in the North.

These stories share similarities with folklore, especially the risks of mistranslation–the same that makes some of us remember the opening of "The Gettysburg Address" as talking about "our Forefathers." But writing them down risks even more, the sense of dramatic immediacy that recaptures the quality of the storyteller's performance and thus the drama of the experience being recounted. In the 1860s everything would have been read aloud and with appropriate performance. Just as in the theater, the play on the stage is not the play on the page, neither is the newspaper story.

Still, we can see the substance of the soldiers'

Harper's Monthly
August 1861

VALIANT MEN "DAT FITE MIT SIGEL"

concerns. The early days of the war saw even deprivation as a source of fun, but mostly comic relief came from raw recruits, officers, civilians, or troops from other regions. As deprivation worsened, stories about "eating so much mule meat made their ears grow" became more nostalgic than nauseous. A writer in *Harper's Magazine* pointed out that there is not one letter's difference between man's *laughter* and *manslaughter*. One private recalled that "the roughest jokes," he ever heard, "were under heavy fire." "We laugh at everything," he said. And as the war went on the laughter grew more nervous. Where earlier the fun had been from wordplay or silliness, absurdity and irony came to mark the soldiers' stories and those by the folks they left behind – householders and farmers subject to total war. Religious authority along with absurd stupidity come under increasing ridicule– "Are you supported by divine Authority?" "No, damn it all, by the 9th New Jersey!"

In a war of unprecedented casualties, death itself became a fit subject for fun, as when a bullet takes off a trooper's head and his companion cries, "Don't let the old boy bleed on the biscuits!" This is not the gallows humor of folklore, but bears the stamp of authenticity familiar to subsequent generations of GIs for whom the unthinkable became routine. So, too, with the civilian sufferers, as those in Tennessee who were asked (as became routine all over) to save human waste for making gunpowder. My venerable friend Rev. Huston Horn, writing a biography of General Polk, found this verse stashed at the end of the reel of microfilmed Polk papers:

> "Written on reading Jon Harelson's eloquent appeal in the Selma papers for chambre-lye, begging families to preserve it for him, and promising to send his cart round every morning. He was first appointed chief of the Nitre Bureau. The Boys had all left town for the front in Virginia, and none but families were left in Selma to pee for him.

> Jon Harelson, Jon Harelson,
> You are a funny creature;
> You've given to this civil war
> A new and useful feature.

a Verdi. stockade

Harper's Weekly 4 May 1861

Organ-ized guard of grinders.

Musical artillery-firing a 40 cracketter.

The Maestro conducting
a siege in persona.

THE MUSIC FOR THE TIMES.

Orchestral lancers a la Verdi.!

Grand charge of Tromboners

You let us know, while every man,
Is bound to be a fighter,
The women, bless them, can be put
To making lots of nitre.

Jon Harelson, Jon Harelson,
When did you get the notion
To send your barrels round our streets,
And fill them with that lotion?

We thought the ladies did enough
At sewing shirts and kissing,
But you have put the lovely dears
To patriotic pissing.

Jon Harelson, Jon Harelson,
Can't you suggest a neater
And faster method for our folks
To make up your salt-petre?
Indeed the thing's so very odd,
Gunpowder like and cranky,
That, when a lady lifts her shift,
She shoots a horrid Yankee!"

By war's end, this community effort had failed and few could boast either pot or window to throw it out of. After the war, General Daniel Harvey Hill gathered Confederate recollections and published them in his magazine, *The Land We Love*, including a section devoted to wartime sayings and stories, before memory had a chance to enshroud them in romantic haze. South Carolina editor Felix de Fontaine had done the same thing during the war, a touchstone for the stories' authenticity. Thanks to their efforts, along with the surviving newspapers in such repositories as the celebrated Nicholson Collection in the Huntington Library, we can sample a substantial stock of Southern material to compare with the many more from the North.

What these samples show is simply that Lincoln was right in saying that the things which divide us are transient, those that unite us permanent. The bond is our common humanity, even when displayed raw as in these stories of man's laughter. In preparing them, I am ever grateful to the Huntington Library for material support as well as permis-

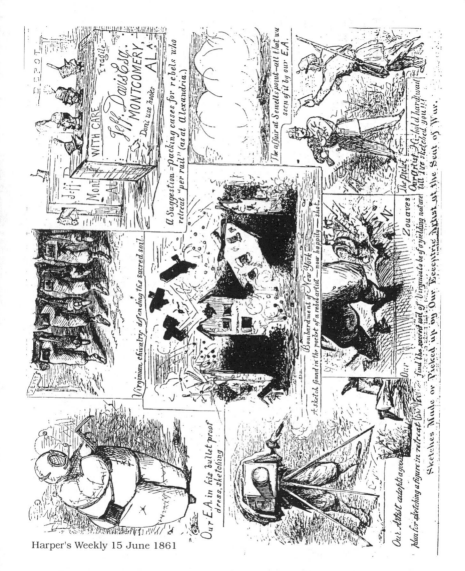

Harper's Weekly 15 June 1861

sion to exploit the boundless resources here–not least the advice and counsel of resident scholars like James McPherson, Huston Horn, and Martin Ridge, veteran--of more wars than one.

PMZ
Huntington Library
December 15, 1995

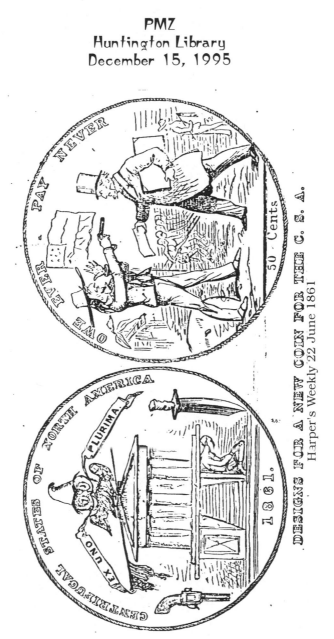

1861

A deputation of sixteen Virginians and eight Marylanders visited the President on the 21st of April and demanded a cessation of hostilities until after the session of Congress! Mr. Lincoln, of course, declined the proposition. One of the delegation said that 75,000 Marylanders would contest the passage of troops over her soil; to which the President replied that he presumed there was room enough on her soil to bury 75,000 men.[1]

Rev. Mr. Beattie, of the Bethel [Baptist Church] at Cleveland, Ohio, presented a revolver to one of the soldiers of the Seventh Regiment before his departure with the following injunction: "If you get in a tight place and have to use it, ask God's blessing if you have time, but be sure and not let your enemy get the start of you. You can say, 'Amen' after you shoot."[2]

A bold soldier boy belonging to the Thirteenth New York Regiment writes from Washington to his sister: "I have grown two feet in two days, prefer gunpowder to butter on my bread, and have made arrangements to sleep forever hereafter in a cannon."[3]

"Now what do yer call this 'ere? Is it beef? or mutton? or pork? D'ye suppose I kin eat sech garbage an do half a day's work? I say flesh and blood can't stand it, this starvin' a feller because he's went an felt patriotic an 'listed hisself for the wars! Now suppose one of 'em chaps . . . the ones who've got all the tin was kep' on a cracker a day, with spiled bacon as us boys have been! Only, I'd jes' like for to feed 'em, and show 'em how long it 'ud be Afore they got fat and jolly on the Red Tape that's starvin me!'"[4]

A day or two since, a couple of Firemen Zouaves strolled over the Long Bridge into Virginia, when they came across a small party of Secession scouts. One of the "Lambs," beckoning a scout aside, asked him if he belonged to the "chivalry." The scout replying in the affirmative, the "Lamb" proceeded to examine him very minutely, taking off his cap, lifting up the skirts of his coat, etc.; after which he

Harper's Weekly 22 June 1861

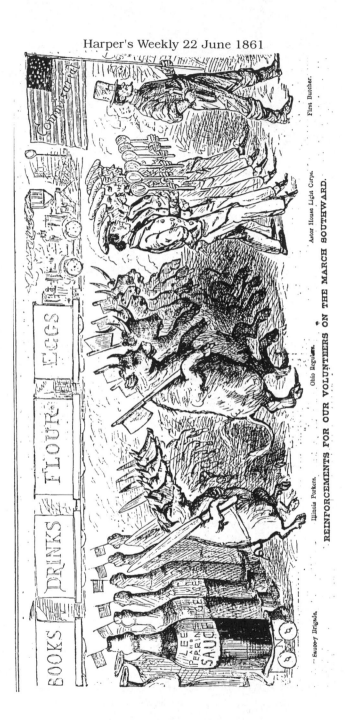

REINFORCEMENTS FOR OUR VOLUNTEERS ON THE MARCH SOUTHWARD.

turned, as if disappointed, to his companion with, "Why, damn it, Joe, he's just like other men!"[5]

A countryman was in the town of Lumpkin, Georgia last week, and someone asked him how he liked the war news. He replied, "Very well." "Are you to go?" he was asked. "Yes," he replied. "Are you not afraid?" "No. If I should see a Yankee with his gun levelled at me, I would draw out my pocketbook and ask him what he would take for his gun, and right there the fight would end."[6]

One of the "contraband" who has found his way to Boston with the returning troops and who is some 14 years old, relates his experience on the battlefield: "I was drivin' an ambulance when a musket-ball came and killed my horse; and den, pretty soon the shell came along, and he blow my wagon all to pieces, and den I got off!"[7]

One of the Fire Zouaves, who had been in the Battle of Bull Run and vamoosed very soon thereafter, was recognized near Washington Market in this city a day or two ago. "What the devil are you doing here?" asked the acquaintance when he recognized him, "got leave of absence?" "No," tendered the Zouave, "I got word to 'fall back' at Bull Run and nobody has told me to halt, so I kept on retreatin' ever since and got away here."[8]

In the Battle at Bull Run, a soldier around whom the cannon shot were flying particularly thick, on seeing one strike and bury itself in a bank near him, sprang to the hole it had scooped out, remarking, "Shoot away! You can't hit twice in the same place." At that instant, another shot struck at a few feet distance, almost covering the fellow with sand and gravel. Emerging from what had so nearly become his grave, he continued the unfinished sentence: "But you can come so pesky near it that the first hole is uncomfortable."[9]

Yesterday one raw captain of a rural company . . . wanted to leave the squad he was drilling for a moment, and brought them to the "rest" in this style: "Squad, break ranks! but if any of you leave your places till I come back, I will have you put in the guardhouse!"[10]

Harper's Monthly June 1861

VOLUNTEERING DOWN DIXIE.

A cartoon caption in weekly series, "Humors of the War," this one depicts two Confederate troopers slouched under a tree along a river bank: "This is the way a southern gentleman has to fight for his country, is it?" "Breakfast! Why, I'velived two days, now, on an old boot, and a darn poor boot at that!"[11]

At the Lewinsville skirmish, Col. Sol Meredith of Wayne County, Indiana, commanding the 19th Indiana, was at the head of his men as they were formed in line of battle under fire of the enemy. As the shells exploded over them, his boys would involuntarily duck their heads. The colonel saw their motions, and in a pleasant way exhorted them, as he rode along the line, to hold up their heads and act like men. He turned to speak to one of his officers, and at that moment an 18-pounder shell burst within a few yards of him, scattering the fragments in all directions. Instinctively he jerked his head almost to the saddle bow, while his horse squatted with fear. "Boys," said he as. he raised up and reined his steed, "you may dodge the large ones!"[12]

(A squad of Indiana volunteers scouting the mountains found an old woman in a log cabin:) After the usual salutations one of them asked her: "Well, old lady, are you a secessionist?" "No," was her answer. "Are you a unionist?" "No." "What are you, then?" "A Baptist– and always have been."[13]

(Explaining soldiers' talk:) The word "arms" has been distorted into "uum," like the last groan of a dying cat, and in place of "march" we hear "utch." A tent is "the canvas," a sword is a "toad-sticker," and any of the altered patterns of muskets are known as "howitzers." Mess beef is "oolt horse." Coffee is "boiled rye," vegetables are "cow feed," and butter is "strong grease." "Bully" is the highest term of commendation, while dissent is expressed in the remark, "I don't see it."[14]

Bishop General (Leonidas) Polk is falling into the habit of using strong expressions for a man who seceded from the clerical profession. It is stated on the authority of a gentleman who was present, that a note of inquiry was sent down to Columbus by General Grant, after the fight at

Harper's Weekly 17 August 1861

PENNSYLVANIA BEEF CONTRACTOR. "Want Beefsteak? Good Gracious, what is the World coming to? Why, my Good Fellow, if you get Beefsteak, how on earth are Contractors to live? Tell me that,"

Harper's Weekly
7 September 1861

THE NATIONAL PURSE THE BEST AUXILIARY.

Belmont, in which the action was mentioned as a "skirmish." The Bishop General, on reading it, exclaimed, "Skirmish! hell and damnation! I'd like to know what he calls a "battle!"[15]

About the time of the battle of Springfield, one of the Dubuque officers (of the First Iowa) whose duty it was to furnish the guards with a password for the night, gave the word "Potomac." A German on guard, not understanding distinctly the difference between the "Bs" and "Ps," understood it to be "Bottomic," and this on being transferred to another, was corrupted to "Buttermilk." Soon afterwards, the officer who had given the word wished to return through the lines, and approaching a sentinel was ordered to halt (and give the password). He gave "Potomac." "Nicht right. You don't pass mit me dis way." "But this is the word, and I will pass." "No. You stand.'" At the same time placing a bayonet at his breast in a manner that told Mr. Officer that "Potomac" didn't pass in Missouri. "What is the word, then?" "Buttermilk, damn you." "Well, then 'buttermilk damn you.'" "Dat is right. Now you pass mit yourself all about your pizness."[16]

A Connecticut soldier writes home that the commissary at Annapolis has given the boys so much mule meat that the ears of the whole regiment have grown 3 1/2 inches since their arrival.[17]

An Irishman from Battle Creek, Michigan, was at Bull Run battle and was somewhat startled when the head of his companion on the left hand was knocked off by a cannon ball. A few moments after, however, a spent ball broke the fingers of his comrade on the right! The latter threw down his gun and yelled with pain, when the Irishman rushed to him, exclaiming, "Blasht your soul, you owld woman, shtop cryin'; you make more noise about it than the man that lost his head!"[18]

(Colonel of a Mississippi regiment taken prisoner at Bull Run comments on Confederate troops in battle:) "I never in my life saw a set of men so badly scared as ours were on that occasion– except yours." [19]

(Cartoon of Confederate privates in bivouac, dog is

THE SECESHERS' TARGET.

"Our Artillery are improving rapidly in their Firing; they practice constantly at Targets."—*Rebel Paper.*

AN AFFECTIONATE TESTIMONIAL TO THE PENNSYLVANIA FOURTH, AND TO VARIAN'S (N. Y.) FIELD BATTERY.

stealing food:) "I say, Jim, look out there! That dog is after your rations!" "Never mind. I'll bet five dollars he can't eat 'em!"[20]

Let me tell you an anecdote that was told at our camp fire (Camp Defiance, Cairo): A number of professional loafers were sitting around the stove in the barroom of a country tavern, and one of them was recounting his adventures and "hairbreadth escapes." He said that once while skating on the river, he was so unfortunate as to get into an airhole. He went under, and the momentum of his body carried him on till he came to another airhole, when he fortunately rose to the surface and was rescued. "Singular, wasn't it?" said he; "I came up just where there was an airhole!" And he looked around in a manner that intimated that was the place where the astonishment was to come in. At this juncture, an old fellow, semi-saturated with "dog's nose," turned to the skater and with an air of patronizing encouragement said, "Johnny, that's the best thing you could ha' done."[21]

Notes

[1] *Rebellion Record*, I.ii.54 and *New York Times* 27 April.

[2] *New York Evening Post* 10 May.

[3] *Boston Transcript* 22 May.

[4] "The Volunteer's Soliloquy," *Vanity Fair* 3 (25 May) 249.

[5] *Leslie's Illustrated Newspaper* 12 (25 May) 19 quoting the Washington Star.

[6] *Rebellion Record* I.i. 2(May) 294 quoting Montgomery (Alabama) *Weekly Post*.

[7] *Boston Journal* 3 August.

[8] *New York Tribune*, 6 August.

[9] *New York World*, 13 August.

[10] *Harpers Monthly* 23 (August), 425.

[11] *Vanity Fair* 4(September 14), 126.

[12] Galesburg, Illinois *Democrat* 17 October.

[13] *New York Tribune* 29 October.

[14] *Cincinnati Commercial* 20 November.

[15] *Boston Evening Transcript* 6 December.

[16] *Leslie's Illustrated*, 7 December, 43.

[17] *Boston Traveller* 14 December.

[18] *Harpers Weekly*, 25 December, 828.

Blue and Gray Laughing

Harper's Weekly
7 September 1861

"THE RIGHT SPIRIT."

LANKY. "What are you going to the War for, JIM? You can't fight; you're too fa:
JIM. "Well, if I can't fight, I can't RUN and disgrace myself, any way.

Harper's Weekly
7 September 1861

Costume suggested for the Brave STAY-AT-HOME LIGHT GUARD

[19] *Frank Leslie's Illustrated Weekly,* 28 December, 85.
[20] *Vanity Fair,* 28 December, 286.
[21] *Knickerbocker Magazine,* December, 544.

Blue and Gray Laughing

1862

One of the zealous chaplains of the Army of the Potomac called on a colonel, noted for his profanity, to talk about the religious interests of his men. He was politely received and beckoned to a seat on a chest. "Colonel," said he, "you have one of the finest regiments in the army." "I think so," replied the Colonel. "Do you think you pay sufficient attention to religious instruction of your men?" "Well, I don't know," replied the Colonel. "A lively interest has been awakened in the -- regiment. The Lord has blessed the labors of his servants, and ten men have been already baptized." "Is that so, your honor?" asked the Colonel. "Yes, sir." "Sergeant," said the Colonel to the attending orderly, "have fifteen men detailed immediately to be baptized. I'll be damned if I'll be outdone in any respect."[1]

A member of Captain Bushnell's company in the 42nd was about to bite a cartridge when a musketball struck the cartridge from his fingers. Coolly facing the direction from which the shot came, he took out another cartridge and exclaimed: "You can't do that again, old fellow!"[2]

An inquiry should be instituted as to how many of these double-acting shooting irons (Belgian muskets) we have in the country–"double acting" because about equally dangerous at either end. A good story is told of one of our Illinois colonels, who was heard praising the arm. He says: "In platoon firing with the Belgian musket, I can tell what I cannot with any other arm, and that is, how many pieces have been fired." "How can you tell that?" "Oh, I count the men on the ground. It never deceives me. It is 'fire and fall back– flat.'"

The bayonet, too, is a novelty: a soft iron affair, apparently designed to coil around the enemy as it is introduced, thus taking him prisoner.[3]

It is said that the Army of the Potomac is going to advance as soon as the Rebels get out of the way.[4]

An Irishman enlisted in the 75th Regiment so as to

Harper's Weekly
7 September 1861

AN AFFECTIONATE TESTIMONIAL TO THE PENNSYLVANIA
FOURTH, AND TO VARIAN'S (N. Y.) FIELD BATTERY.

be near his brother, who was in the 74th.[5]

I have had some fun hugging Union and Secession Girls; they say they like to have a Yankee hug them, and you can bet I was no ways backward after being away from the fair sex for some months. I went in on double Quick.[6]

(A "lady in the interior" writes:) Our soldier boys were about to set off for the seat of war. At the station a large crowd of friends had gathered, and there was the usual amount of kissing, weeping, embracing, and leave-taking. A loud-voiced man was entertaining a group of ladies with his conversation, and he remarked, as one of the soldiers' sweet little wives was passing, "If I was going to the war, and any of my friends should come down to the station to see me off, I would shoot them." The little woman looked up and very quietly said, "Oh, don't fret – you wouldn't have a chance to fire once!"[7]

Some time after we arrived in Virginia we heard that quite a large number of letters for the regiment were detained at Indianapolis for the postage. While passing through the camp one day, I overheard a couple of soldiers conversing about those letters. One inquired, "what would be done with them?" The other replied, "I suppose they will be sent to the dead-letter office, and after we get killed we can get them.[8]

In the Third Regiment Wisconsin Volunteers it is a rule that no soldier can leave camp without a pass.
The chaplain one day was distributing tracts. Among others was one headed, "Come, sinners, come!" Soon after, the tract was picked up in camp, and under the heading was penciled, "Can't do it! Colonel Ruger won't sign my pass!"[9]

(After the battle of Leesburg) I passed General Wigfall on my return from dinner and asked him if there was any news.
"No," said he, "I don't believe we have been whipped since dinner. I expect, though, to hear of another defeat in the next five minutes."[10]

In Smyth County, Virginia, we learn one man, in

YANKEE VOLUNTEERS MARCHING INTO DIXIE
"YANKEE DOODLE KEEP IT UP. YANKEE DOODLE DANDY."
J.H. Ayford's 1862

enrolling himself (with hopes of exemption from draft), wrote opposite his name, "One leg too short." The next man that came in thought he would make his better and wrote opposite his name, "Both legs too short!"[11]

Shoes furnished (Pennsylvania troops) were generally much too large for the wearers. This fact occasioned much merriment and some inconvenience. A raw recruit in Colonel Owen's regiment was being put through the squad drill when the following colloquy took place: "Sergeant": "Why don't ye mind the others there, Patrick Kelly? There ye've been standin' like a solapeen ever since ye come out, and niver once faced to the right or left! Shure an' I'll arrest ye! D'ye mind that?" Private: "Ye're mistaken altogether, sergeant. Shure an' ye've bin lookin' at me shoes. Divil a bit can I turn them around!"[12]

Scene at the Park Barracks, New York: *Dramatis Personae*, a sick and wounded but good looking soldier and an anxious lady nurse in search of a subject: Lady Nurse: "My poor fellow, can I do anything for you?"

Soldier (emphatically): "No, ma'm, nothin'!"

Lady Nurse: "I should like to do something for you. Shall I not sponge your face and brow for you?"

Soldier (despairingly): "You may if you want to very bad; but you'll be the fourteenth lady as has done it this blessed mornin'."[13]

Two Kentucky regiments met face to face at the Battle of Shiloh and fought each other with terrible resolution, and it happened that one of the Federal soldiers wounded and captured his brother, and after handing him back, began firing at a man near a tree, when the captured brother called to him and said, "Don't shoot there anymore—that's father!"[14]

Our regiment (Tenth Maine) is guarding the Baltimore and Ohio Railroad from the Relay House to Annapolis Junction, and our men are stationed at short intervals for the length of ten miles. To carry provisions to the men we have an engine and one car, which go up every morning. A sentry on duty is expected to "present arms" only to the field or staff officers as they pass. It was noticed by the officer in charge that one sentry always brought his piece to a "present arms" as the dinner train passed. He said to him, "Why do you 'present arms'? We are not the Colonel." The answer was, "Do you think I care more for my Colonel than for my dinner?"[15]

It is the custom of the Colonel of our regiment (Eighty-fifth Pennsylvania) to make the rounds every night in person and satisfy himself that every sentinel is at his post and doing his duty. A few nights ago, while in discharge of that self-imposed duty, he approached a post and received the challenge as usual, "Who comes there?" "Friend with a countersign," was the reply. Here the poor sentinel was at a loss. The rest of his instructions had been forgotten. The Colonel is a very particular man and insists that everything shall be done exactly right. So, after spending considerable time in the endeavor to impress the role upon the mind of the sentinel, suggested that he would act as the sentinel while the other should impersonate the Colonel. "Blinky"-- for such was his surname in the regiment– moved a few paces and then turned to approach the Colonel. "Who comes there?" challenged the Colonel. "Why– Blinky. Don't you know me, Colonel?" This was too much for even so patient and forbearing a man as Colonel Howell. The gun was handed over, and the Colonel passed on to the next post.[16]

In our army at the West, one of the officers, whose duty it was to furnish the guards with a password for the one night, gave the word "Potomac." A German guard, not understanding distinctly the difference between the B's and P's, understood it to be "Bottomic," and this being transferred to another was corrupted to "Buttermilk." Soon afterward, the officer who had given the word wished to return through the lines and, approaching a sentinel, was ordered to halt, and the word demanded. He gave "Potomac." "Nicht right. You don't pass mit me dis way." "But this is the word, and I will pass." "No. You stay," at the same time placing a bayonet at his breast.

"What is the word, then?"

"Buttermilk."

"Well, then, 'Buttermilk.'"

"Dat is right. Now you pass mit yourself all about your pizness."

Lovie the artist records this verse at Lick Creek Bottom between Pittsburg Landing and Monterey:
This road is impassable,
Not even jackassable.[17]

Patrick Conway is a private in Company E, 6th Regiment Iowa Volunteers, from Monroe City. While stationed at Sedalia, Missouri, a peddler came into camp with the usual cry, "Pins, combs, thread, buttons!" etc. etc., and threw down his baggage close to Pat's tent. Pat eyed him a moment, rose on his feet, and addressed him with, "What ye doin' here with old trumpery? Leave here, or by the holy mither of Moses, I'll be after kickin' ye out of the camp! Leave, damn ye!" The peddler thought that discretion was the better part of valor and left.

After he had gone, one of the boys said, "Pat, why did you drive that fellow off? I wished to buy some of his goods." Pat answered, "And what the divil do I care? Didn't Captain Henry Saunders order me from Albia to St. Louis and from St. Louis to Springfield, and then back to Sedalia, and haven't I been ordered about for the last six months, and during all that time haven't had the pleasure of ordering a single man before? And d'ye suppose I am goin' to let sich a chance as this pass without ordering the spalpeen away?"[18]

Mother Lincoln's Melodies:

McClellan came to our town,
And he was wondrous wise,
He jumped into a 'skeeter swamp,
And started telling lies;
And when he found his lies were out,
With all his might and main,
He changed his base to another place,
And began to lie again.

Yankee was a bad man,
Yankee was a thief
Yankee came to my house and stole all my beef;
I went to Yankee's house,
Yankee he had fled,
Caught him on the battlefield,
and there I killed him dead.[19]

Harper's Weekly
4 October 1862

THE REBEL CHIVALRY

As the Fancy of "My Maryland" painted them

As "My Maryland" found them.

McClellan was Lieutenant, on service at Fort Yuma in the very earliest California days, when potatoes were worth $3,000 apiece and everything else eatable at the same rate. Lieutenant Derby, whom all the world knows as "John Phoenix," of funny fame, was invited to go up to the fort and dine with Mac under the promise that there would be dinner served that was a great favorite with the future Commander-in-chief. Derby smacked his lips some days in advance, good things not being over abundant, and at the appointed hour made his appearance in the fort. Dinner was announced, and a rousing bowl of boiled rice was set upon the table, flanked by a tumbler of mustard.

Derby stared in astonishment, and at last, seeing McClellan about to fall to, demanded, "Where the devil's the dinner?" "Here, my boy," answered Mac blandly, giving the mustard a stir, "rice and mustard. Splendid thing–try it." Derby curled his nose in horror and disappointment. "Rice and mustard! Pah! I never eat rice! I can't eat rice! I don't like rice!"

"Don't like rice?" responded Mac, in astonishment. "Don't like rice! Well, I'm confounded sorry, my boy. However, make the best of it–help yourself to the mustard."[20]

Between McClellan and his dead
This difference arises:
They fertilizer make,'tis said
And he makes fertile lies, sirs.[21]

Our commissaries seem to think that by feeding soldiers on dough, they make them doughty warriors. They mistake, and the men miss steak.[22]

[Maj. Gen. John] Pope has been sent West to attend to the Indians. If true to his former instincts and practices, he will increase rather than diminish the race.[23]

Maryland has been so long fermenting in the yeasty waves of civil strife, that it may be presumed she is *prepared* by this time for a general rising. If this is not soon manifested, we must conclude that the flower of her youth is not of the same family brand, and her cake is emphatically all dough.[24]

(from "Foot-Cavalry Chronicle":)
1. Man that is born of woman and enlisteth in Jackson's army is of few days and short rations.
4. Much soldiering hath made him sharp; yea, even the sole of his shoe is in danger of being cut through.
7. He fireth his Minie ball at the dead hour of night, and the camp is aroused and formed in line–when, to his mess he cometh bearing a fine porker, which he declareth so resembleth a Yankee that he was compelled to pull the trigger.[25]

> Said Braggadocio Pope one day, the day
> Before he from Manassas ran away,
> "In many fights with Southrons have I been,
> But never yet the foeman's face have seen";
> For once Bragg told the truth– the fact was so,
> For never yet he fairly *faced* the foe.[26]

A telegraph operator was taken prisoner by a gang of guerillas in West Virginia, and the captain offered to spare his life on condition of his taking the oath to support the Southern Confederacy. He promptly replied that if, after a whole life's hard work and the use of more oaths than it was pleasant to reflect upon, he had been unable to support himself, how could it be expected that he could support the Confederacy taking only one?[27]

A correspondent writing from "Camp in the Woods, near Corinth": As we sat this noon under an arbor, sheltering ourselves from the intense sun here, the distant boom and growl of a '32'[lb. shot] at regular intervals reminded us of the usual national salute at meridian on the Fourth of July. The Lieutenant spoke up, "What's that, Cap'n?" "It's customary to fire a national salute at meridian," I replied.
"Meridian? Meridian? Whare's that, Cap'n? I've never heered of any such place about yere," replied the Lieutenant.[28]

(A correspondent from Pennsylvania:) A Captain of one of our Harrisburg companies had hard work in bringing his men up to military standard of promptness and efficiency. One of his men was uniformly late in making his appearance. But when the morning came that they were to march to meet the foe, Jinks was the first man on the ground. He saluted his astonished captain, who congratulated him on his early appearance . . . . "Why, corporal Jinks, I'm glad to see you! You're first at last. You're early of late. You were always behind before."[29]

(A soldier in the South writes:) In our regiment there is a rule requiring every member "who has not conscientious scruples against attending Protestant worship" to be present at service on the Sabbath. A few days after this order was issued, a fatigue party was dragging a truck loaded with a piece of artillery. The load was heavy and some of the men were taking a rest. Presently one of them seized hold of the rope and cried out "All who hain't, conscientious scruples against work lay hold here!"[30]

Here is a story about Price and Polk, which is much relished in the armies of the Southwest, and to the truth of which every man will swear. While Price and Polk were at Corinth, a captain in command of the pickets came to General Price's tent, in which General Polk happened at the time to be, and said the enemy's pickets were too strong for him, what must he do?
"Take your whole company," replied General Price.
In five minutes the Captain returned and said the enemy's pickets were too strong for him.
"Take a battalion," replied General Price.
Five minutes had not elapsed before the Major in command returned with the same statement– the enemy's pickets were too strong for him.
"Order out a regiment," said General Price in tones of excitement to one of his aides.
The Colonel of the regiment ordered out returned in about five minutes saying the enemy's pickets were too strong for him.
"Order a brigade!" thundered Price to his aides
In less than five minutes the Brigadier General returned with the same story– the enemy's pickets were too strong for him.
General Price, now thoroughly aroused, uttered a

Harper's Monthly June 1862   GEN'L STUART'S RAID TO "WHITE HOUSE," VA.

violent expletive and declared he would go in person to see what these mysterious statements about the enemy's pickets could possibly mean.

General Polk, also much mystified and excited, waited in the tent to hear General Price's report. He had but five minutes to wait before General Price returned at full speed with the same story–the enemy's pickets were too strong for him.

General Polk, utterly amazed, demanded an explicit report.

"To tell the truth, General," said Price, "I came back because I was scared." "What did you see?"

"I saw," replied General Price, "a colossal white figure which seemed at least twenty feet high. It strode towards me with threatening gesticulations. I waited until it was within five feet of me, and then fired every barrel of both my revolvers into it. Seeing that my bullets produced no effect upon it, I–to be honest–turned and ran as hard as I could." More astonished than ever, General Polk inquired, "Did it speak to you?"

"Yes," replied General Price, "it did speak to me."

"Well? What did it say?"

"It said that it was–" and here General Price hesitated.

"'It said that it was' what?" inquired General Polk.

"It said that it was a damned long time between drinks!"[31]

The explosion of a rifled 125-pounder occurred at Columbus, Kentucky on the 10th of November last year. . . . Major Rucker was blown from the embankment that surrounded the gun. When he had partially recovered his senses, he felt someone beside him. The air was so densely filled with smoke and powder that the sufferers could not see, and breathing was painful and difficult.

Rucker asked who he was that lay beside him. "I am General Polk," was the almost inaudible answer.

"This is hell, ain' it, General?" inquired Rucker.

"It smells like it, I believe," answered the General.[32]

A member of the regimental staff of the 8th Alabama Regiment, lying at Richmond, lost himself one morning in the woods. Coming upon the Union pickets, he was brought to a stand, and mistaking the character of the men, inquired for his regiment. The pickets directed him to the colonel's tent for information. He went there and was told to consider himself a prisoner. He merely replied, "A damned funny mistake of our picket to send me the wrong way."[33]

Tall Young Texan (at Jackson, Mississippi): "We have plenty of arms, plenty of provisions, plenty of everything. Good Lord! what splendid boots those are!"

Yank prisoner: "Are boots scarce in the Confederacy?"

"I paid $25 for these shoes," and he pointed to a pair of flimsy pumps he wore.

"Why, don't you make leather in the Confederacy?"

"Don't know how– but they are making clay pipes in Alabama!"[34]

When the Union soldiers entered the rebel fortifications at Mill Spring, one of them discovered a barrel which proved to contain apple brandy. Pulling out the corn cob from the bung hole, he turned it up and filled his canteen. While doing this, one of Bob McCook's skirmishers came in and said, "Vat you gets dere?"

The soldier replied that it appeared to be pretty fair apple brandy, upon which the Dutchman ran to the door calling out furiously, "Hans! Heinrich! Schnapps! See here!"

Then rushed in a squad of his comrades, and the brandy was transferred to their canteens in a twinkling. The soldier was fond of a joke and remarked seriously, "Boys, this is a doctor's shop, and there might be strychnine in that brandy."

The thirsty teutons paused a moment, when one of them exclaimed, "Py Got! Hans, I tell you vat I does. I trinks some, and if it don't kill me, den you trinks mitout no danger."

He then took a long pull at his canteen, smacked his lips, and said, "All right, boys, go ahead!"[35]

An orderly rode rapidly across the bridge and said to General Jackson, "I am ordered by General McLaws to report to you that General McClellan is within six miles, with an immense army.

Jackson took no notice of the orderly apparently and

continued his conversation. But when the orderly turned away, Jackson called after him, "Has McClellan any baggage train or drove of cattle?"

"He has, sir," replied the orderly.

"Very well," he said, "my men are hungry, and we can whip any army that is followed by a drove of cattle."[36]

Jerry Ballou, a decent old man, gave us a supper, a good bed, and a chance to nurse my wounded man. As we rode up, his little daughter looked curiously at me.

"Paw, is that a Yankee?"

"Yes, little dear," said I, "and if I had known I was coming to make you a visit, I should have worn my horns."

The child looked wonders at me, and eyeing me from head to foot, innocently remarked, "Well, I don't see but you look like people when you hain't got your horns on."[37]

During the battle of Antietam, broken railroad iron, blacksmith's tools, hammers, chisels, etc., were fired at us from rebel cannons. Some of these missiles made a peculiar noise, resembling "which-away, which-away," by which our men came to distinguish them from regular shot and shell, and as they heard them approaching they would cry, "Turkey! turkey coming!" and fall flat to avoid them. One of the artillerists, a German, when he saw the tools falling around him exclaimed, "My Got! we shall have the blacksmith's shop to come next!"[38]

At Paducah, Kentucky where Federals let mules forage for themselves, many were rustled by speculators. Two privates of the 14th Illinois disguised themselves as farmers to retrieve them. The boys rode furiously into camp with their shrieking retinue, and reported to General Smith "Well, boys, what luck?" asked the General.

"We got 'em good, sure, and more, too."

"Ah!" said the General, "how many did you get?"

"Well, about forty, I reckon–hain't counted 'em yet."

"But that is more than we lost. You didn't steal any, I hope?"

"Steal!" exclaimed the soldier, "Kristopher! *Steal!* No, sirree, but you see we didn't have time to put up the bars after we got ourn out, and the damned things would foller!"

The General sternly lectured the soldier for using

THE LAST DITCH AT LAST.—Scene near Corinth

Harper's Weekly 5 July 1862

profane language in the presence of a general officer. The soldier took the lecture quite uneasily, twirling his hat nervously, and, when the General concluded, apologized: "You see, General, we've had to cuss the damned things all day to get 'em into camp, and it's devilish hard to quit all of a sudden."

The boys declared, as they closed the door, that such a pious old cuss had no business to be "round among soldiers."[39]

A New York Zouave in one of his scouting expeditions captured a very fine horse. In a few days the owner came into camp and claimed the animal.

"The critter's confiscated," said Zoo-Zoo.

"But I'm not a rebel," said the man, "I'm Union, and the Government protects my property."

"Ya-as," drawled the Zouave, "I wouldn't give much for your loyal rebel's sentiment. It's too elastic." "But I've taken the oath," persisted the man. "Can't help if you have," replied Zoo-Zoo coolly, "the horse hain't, and I can't release him!"[40]

A rebel soldier tells the following story: Not long since, a lot of us were quartered in several wooden tenements, and in the inner room of one lay the corpse of a young secesh officer awaiting burial.

The news soon spread to a village not far off. Down came a sentimental, and not bad looking specimen of a Virginia dame. "Let me kiss him for his mother!" she cried, as I interrupted her progress, "Do let me kiss him for his mother!"

"Kiss whom?"

"The dear little lieutenant, the one who lies dead within Point him out to me, sir, if you please. I never saw him, but—oh!"

I led her through a room in which a Union prisoner, a lieutenant from Philadelphia, lay stretched out on an upturned trough fast asleep. Supposing him to be the article sought for, she rushed up, exclaiming, "Let me kiss him for his mother," and approached her lips to his forehead. What was her amazement when the corpse ardently clasped its arms around her, returned the salute vigorously and exclaimed: "Never mind the old lady, Miss; go it on your own

Harper's Weekly
2 August 1862

SCENE, FIFTH AVENUE

CAPTAIN DASH, of the Army of the Potomac, absent on Furlough, calls upon his adored: WAITER. "No, Sar; MISS 'LIZA'S not to home, and, Sar, she say she won't be to home you 'till *Richmond is took.* Mornin', Sar."

account. I haven't the slightest objection." [41]

At Mountain Run, a small branch which joins the Rappahannock, General Wilcox was riding in advance of the army, attended by a single trooper, when the latter discovered one of the Yankee pickets peeping over the top of a boulder. "Shall I bring him down?" said the soldier, raising his piece to his shoulder? "No," replied the General, "the distance is too great. Better not waste your powder."
Hardly were the words out of his mouth before "whizz"–a Minie ball flew within three inches of the General's ear and lodged in the bank behind him." "You may shoot," said Wilcox.[42]

A gentleman who had been a Major General in the militia when he was drafted reported himself at headquarters with his regimentals on, ready for duty, to take command of any division that should be assigned to him. But he was exceedingly shocked and astonished when informed that they were not drafting Major Generals, and that he was only a private.[43]

A soldier from Rhode Island, while on picket guard, was rushed by a party of rebel cavalry. Fortunately for the soldier the rains had made the field quite muddy, and the horses slumped through the turf so badly that they could not lessen the distance between them and the fugitive. The picket at last reached the fence, and with one bound landed on the top, intending to give a long spring ahead, but the fence was frail and crumbled beneath his weight. It so chanced that a hog had rooted out a gutter at this place and was lying snoring therein. At the cracking of the fence, his swineship evacuated his hole and scampered, barking, into the underbrush.
Up came the horsemen and, hearing the rustling of the leaves and not doubting it was their prey, dashed through the gap in the fence and, seeing the path in the brush, they put through it after the hog and were soon out of sight.
The next day one of these rebel horsemen was taken prisoner. When our hero saw him, he recognized him at once and sung out:
"I say, old fellow, did you catch that hog yesterday?"

"We did that," retorted the prisoner, "but it wasn't the one we were after."[44]

(Quoting George D. Prentice, *Louisville Journal*): A Northern editor calls Virginia, "The seat of war and the seat of honor." He is making a butt of her.

(Quoting a Norfolk, Virginia newspaper:) While the ladies of this city were recently gathered in cutting out drawers for the soldiers, it appeared that after their labor was concluded, cloth was left for just one leg of the same. The question being raised as to what should be done with this, one of the number promptly responded, "Oh, that will do for use after they get back."[45]

General Howard's right arm was shattered by a ball in one of the recent battles before Richmond, and it was amputated above the elbow. While being borne on a litter he met General Kearney, who had lost his left arm in Mexico. "I want to make a bargain with you, General," said Howard, "that hereafter we buy our gloves together".[46]

While the Indiana clergyman (near Corinth. Mississippi) was offering the concluding prayer, a rifle shot was heard as if from our pickets a mile beyond. The report of the gun was immediately followed by an exclamation from a venerable Hoosier, "Lord, if that's a Union shot, send the bullet straight–an' if it ain't, hit a tree with it!" [47]

At Nashville a very ardent secesh lady, who wished to see Colonel Matthews, was about to pass through the gate, when looking up she beheld the proud flag. Starting back horror struck, she held up her hands and exclaimed to the guard, "Dear me! I can't go under that dreadful Lincoln flag. Is there no other way for me to enter?"
"Yes, madam," promptly replied the orderly, and turning to his comrade, he said, "Here, orderly, bring out that rebel flag and lay it on the ground at the little gate and let this lady walk over it!" [48]

At Pohic Church, the squad from the 63rd Pennsylvania Volunteers had the satisfaction to observe the cautious approach, not of a cow, but a veritable secesher with a cowbell around his neck and a six-shooter stuck in his belt. He came slowly on until within easy range of our men. The sergeant then hailed him and asked where he had rather go–"to hell or to Washington?" "To Washington, I reckon," drawled the secesher. "I ain't clothed for warm weather."[49]

I was stopped by a sentinel, whom I recognized as Private P--, though he did not recognize me. I was asked for the countersign and replied, "Friend with a bottle." The reply was, "Advance bottle and draw stopper."[50]

Notes

[1] *Louisville Journal* 14 January; *Rebellion Record* 4.ii.34
[2] *Cleveland Herald* 16 January; *Rebellion Record* 4.ii.50.
[3] *Chicago Tribune* 20 January; *Rebellion Record* 4.ii.25.
[4] *The Dragoon* (Washington D.C.), 25 February.
[5] *Harpers Monthly,* February, 423.
[6] Ed W. Goble on the Gun Boat *Taylor* at Cairo, Illinois, 5 March, following an expedition up the Tennessee River; Joseph B. Boyd Letters, Cincinnati Historical Society; thanks to Charles Royster.
[7] *Harpers Monthly,* March, 566.
[8] *Ibid.*
[9] *Ibid.*
[10] *New Orleans Crescent,* 7 April, quoted in Nicholson's scrapbook, Huntington accession number 100115, vol. 1, unpaged.
[11] *Atlanta Intelligencer* 10 April.
[12] *Harpers Monthly,* April, 715.
[13] *New York Evening Post* c. 1 May.
[14] *Boston Transcript,* 1 May.
[15] *Harpers Monthly,* May, 857-8.
[16] *Ibid.,* 859.
[17] *Frank Leslie's Illustrated Newspaper,* 14 June, 171
[18] *Harpers Monthly,* July, 280.
[19] *Southern Literary Messenger,* July\August, 509.
[20] *Frank Leslie's Weekly,* 6 September, 375.
[21] *Southern Illustrated News,* 13 September, 2.
[22] *Ibid.*
[23] *Ibid.,* 20 September, 8.
[24] *Ibid.*
[25] *Ibid.,* 8 October, 3.
[26] *Ibid.,* 11 October, 8.

[27] *Harper's Monthly,* September, 571.

[28] *Ibid.,* November, 859.

[29] *Ibid.,* 860.

[30] *Ibid.,* 855.

[31] *Southern Literary Messenger,* November\December, 692.

[32] *Ibid.,* 694.

[33] *Incidents of American Camp Life* (New York: T.R. Dawley, 1862), 60

[34] *Incidents of The War; or the Romance and Realities of Soldier LIfe* (Indianapolis, Asher and Adams, 1862) 6-7.

[35] *IIbid.,* 22-23.

[36] *Ibid.,* 36.

[37] *Ibid.,* 37.

[38] *Ibid.,* 46.

[39] *Ibid.,* 48-49.

[40] *Ibid.,* 60.

[41] *Ibid.,* 62.

[42] *Ibid.,* 68.

[43] *Ibid.,* 72-73.

[44] *Ibid.,* 78-79.

[45] *Ibid.,* 81, 83.

[46] *Incidents of American Camp Life,* 10.

[47] *Ibid.,* 53.

[48] *Ibid.,* 55.

[49] *Ibid.,* 68.

[50] *Ibid.,* 69.

1863

"There is plenty of Rain here to make the mud soft. It is hard to tell the road from the rider for they are all the same coller."[1]

On Saturday at the public reception, a Western paymaster in full Major's attire was introduced and said, "Being here, Mr. Lincoln, I thought I'd call and pay my respects."

"From the complaints of the soldiers," responded the President, "I guess that's about all any of you do pay."[2]

A visitor asked the reason at the convalescent camp for the number of deaths. "You see, sir, the Government laid out a big graveyard, and soldiers always avail themselves of all Government allowances. That's why they die so fast."[3]

The night after the battle of Fredericksburg a council of war was held by General Lee, to which all his Generals of divisions were invited. General Jackson slept through the proceedings, and upon being waked and asked for his opinion, curtly said, "Drive 'em in the river!"[4]

A Charleston, South Carolina paper claims that if General Bragg was near the gates of Heaven and invited in, at the critical moment he would fall back.[5]

When General McCown was commanding at New Madrid, he was greatly alarmed one night at the reported approach of General Pope with a large force to attack the place. At once everything was in commotion, and the General commenced making arrangements for defense. He soon found to his horror that he had no percussion caps for his field pieces. He forthwith dispatched a steamer in hot haste bearing a letter to a colonel, an ordnance officer at Island Number 10, directing him to bring down a supply immediately. The boat reached the island in about an hour. The Colonel was found in a state of wild but sweet inebriety. The letter was delivered to him, and he soon came aboard with a box under his arm, and the steamer returned to New Madrid.[6]

Harper's Weekly
21 March 1863

RAPPAHANNOCK MUD.

PICKET. "Hallo, Comrade! you must find it pretty bad walking on the Roads hereabouts."

MAN IN THE MUD. "Walking? I ain't walking. I'm GENERAL HOOKER's Orderly, and I've got *a right smart horse under me*, I tell you!"

In about fifteen minutes after she landed, the Colonel returned on board and ordered the Captain of the boat to return at once with the boat to Island Number 10. The Captain said he did not think he would go, as he had other orders from Commodore Hollins. "But," said the Colonel, "you must and shall go, for By God, they sent up to me for a box of percussion caps, and I have brought down a box of cigars!"[7]

During the late battle of Fredericksburg, a Zouave from the city of brotherly love, having changed his base from the field of battle to the pontoon bridge, found himself arrested by the guard and requested to show his pass or his wounds. Throwing down his gun and equipments and raising his closed hands to his hips, the irrepressible Zouzou broke through the guard saying, "Let me pass! Let me pass! I'm demoralized!"[8]

One of our Indiana regiments was fiercely attacked by a whole rebel brigade in one of the late battles in Mississippi. The Indianians, unable to withstand such odds, were compelled to fall back about 30 or 40 yards, losing – to the utter mortification of officers and men – their flag, which remained in the hands of the enemy. Suddenly a tall Irishman, a private of the color company, rushed from the ranks across the vacant ground, attacked the squad of rebels who had possession of the conquered flag with his musket, felled several to the ground, snatched the flag from them, and returned safely back to his regiment.

The bold fellow was, of course, immediately surrounded by his jubilant comrades and greatly praised for his gallantry, his captain appointing him to a sergeantry on the spot. But the hero of the occasion cut everything short by the reply, "O, niver mind, Captain, say no more about it. I dropped my whiskey flask among the rebels and fetched that back, and I thought I might just as well bring the flag along!"[9]

The enrolling officer of Salisbury District, Maryland, was very active and thorough in the performance of his duty. One day he went to the house of a countryman and, finding none of the male members of the family at home, made inquiry of an old woman about the number and age of the "males" of the family.

After naming several, the old lady stopped. "Is there no one else?" asked the officer.

"No,"replied the woman,"none except Billy Bray."

"Billy Bray? Where is he?" "He was at the barn a moment ago," said the old lady.

Out went the official, but could not find the man. Coming back, the worthy officer questioned the old lady as to the age of Billy and went away, after enrolling his name among those to be drafted.

The time of the drafting came, and among those on whom the lot fell was Billy Bray. No one knew him. 'Where did he live?" The officer who enrolled him was called on to produce him and, lo and behold, Billy Bray was a jackass! and stands now on the list of drafted men as forming one of the quota of Maryland.[10]

One of our companies is composed of emigres from the fair land of Poland. They were called by the men throughout the camp as "the Poles." One day, as the Colonel was writing in his private office in the barracks, he desired a bundle of papers which were on the top of a high chest. Having nothing at hand to get them down with, he dispatched his orderly, who was one of the Polish gentry, to bring him a long pole. "And mind," said the Colonel, "to bring the longest pole you can find."

Off went the son of Poland and soon returned, bringing with him a tall brother patriot and saying as he entered, "Kollnel, dis is de longest Bole in mine kompany!"[11]

The war has not subdued all the spirit of fun. The Knoxville (Tennessee) *Register* tells a joke connected with the present requisition for conscripts: Some days ago Major Rucker was in conversation with a fair, fat, and buxom widow of an adjoining county when, by accident, she mentioned the age of one of her admirers, stating that he was not quite 39. The Major made a mental note of the fact and soon departed. He went straightway in pursuit of this juvenile admirer of the attractive widow, whom he had before learned was a little more than 40 years of age. When he arrested Mr. Johnson, Rucker stated that he regretted to inform him that he was under the painful necessity of conscripting him. "I have learned," said Rucker, "from Widow –- that you are only 39. She says that you told her so, and I feel it my duty to take you down to Colonel Blake."

"Oh, ah! yes," said Mr. Johnson, "in fact, sir, to tell you the truth, sir, I did lie just a little to Widow, wanted, yes– I wanted to get married– you understand, don't you, Major?"

"I don't understand anything about it," said Rucker, "you must go with me."[12]

One year ago this winter we were stationed at Bird's Point, Missouri. Colonel (now General) Oglesby was then in command of the Eighth Illinois. Well, one day his fife and drum major went out into the woods to practice a new tune. Attracted no doubt by the melody, a fine fat shoat of musical proclivities came near, alas, for the safety of his bacon too near, for our bass-drummer.

But how to get the deceased porker into camp? After considerable discussion an idea strikes the drummer: "We will put him in the drum." "Just the thing, by hokey!"said the fifer. One head was taken out, and the hog stowed in, and our heroes started for their quarters carrying the drum between them.

In the meantime, the regiment went out for dress parade, and the Colonel somewhat vexed at the absence of the principal musicians no sooner saw the gents than, in a voice of reprimand, he ordered them to take their places with the music. The drum-bearers halted, looked at each other, then at the Colonel, but said never a word. The Colonel repeated his order in a style so emphatic that it couldn't be misunderstood.

The dealers in pork felt a crisis had arrived, so the drummer, going up close to the Colonel, in a low voice made him acquainted with the state of affairs, winding up with, "We 'low, Colonel, to bring the best quarter over to your mess." "Sick, eh?" thundered the Colonel, "Why didn't you say so at first?"

A few days since, General Rosecrans was dining with his staff at one of our hotels. He unfortunately tasted the Tennessee butter, when he immediately arose and saluted the plate before him, remarking, "Gentlemen, that butter outranks me!"[13]

In one of the hospitals in the vicinity of Washington,

Harper's Weekly
7 March 1863

THE "ARKANSAS TRAVELER,"
As lately performed with Rapturous Applause by General HINDMAN.

a newly arrived patient by the name of Pat, a veritable son of the Emerald Isle, complained of being quite deaf. The next morning after his arrival the physician, while going his regular rounds prescribing for the different patients in his ward, approached Pat, who was at the time whistling a tune called, "The Irish Washerwoman." The Doctor accosted Pat with, "What is the matter with you?" But Pat didn't seem to hear and continued whistling.

The Doctor, a little bewildered at Pat's impudence, exclaimed rather sharply, "How long have you been in hospital?" Pat said nothing, but made more music than ever. The Doctor by this time began to smell a mouse and screamed out at the top of his voice, "Where did you come from? What hospital were you in before you came here?" But it had not the least impression on Pat, who still continued to whistle. The Doctor, after reading Pat's name on the card at the head of his bed, asked, "Pat, don't you want to go home on furlough?" Pat's eyes glistened for a moment, when he exclaimed, "That's the matter!"[14]

A few days since, a soldier (in the 24th Ohio) in passing to the lower part of the encampment saw two others from his company making a rude coffin. He inquired who it was for.

"John Bunce," said the others.

"Why," replied he," John is not dead yet. It is too bad to make a man's coffin when you don't know if he is going to die or not."

"Don't trouble yourself," replied the others. "Dr. Coe told us to make his coffin, and I guess he knows what he give him."[15]

(Brigadier General Dumont) is famed for his peculiarities, not the least of which is his squeaky, cracked voice, which it would be very hard to imitate. One day, while in command of his regiment before being promoted, an officer of the regiment ventured to suggest something which he thought would greatly add to the discipline and efficiency of the regiment. The General listened to his suggestions very attentively, but at the close answered him in that peculiar tone of his: "I just give you to understand that I command this regiment in my own feeble way."[16]

The 2nd California is now stationed at Fort Lyon, awaiting orders for the States– or "America," as the boys say. The officer in command of the fort has an exquisite daughter, who occasionally attends her father at review. She has a peculiar pronunciation, which was more common in peaceful times.

Wishing to see the boys perform the double-quick, she says, "Pa, please make them 'twot.'" Accordingly the old gentleman made the boys "twot" for the benefit of the fair one– and they "twotted!" [17]

Mrs. W– , an old lady residing in the town of O–– was, just after one of the battles in the Southwest, listening to an account of General Grant's operations in which, among other things, it was stated that he had caused several miles of new road to be constructed and had covered it here and there with corduroy. "Why, bless me!" she exclaimed, "What a waste! Did a body ever hear the like? There's our boys, poor creeturs! some of 'em 'most naked, and the pesky officers using up on them seceshioners roads all that stuff that was sent to make breeches!"[18]

(Marine Sergeant B– talking with marines from the *Monitor*:) "I've been to sea and in fact fell overboard myself once."

"How did that come about?"

"It was down in the Gulf, coming from the West Indies. The Captain didn't like me very well, so he went on and left me. I swam a little– just enough to keep myself afloat– for a number of days."

"But didn't you ever see the vessel again?"

"Oh, yes, but she went home and discharged her cargo and was coming back again. So I swam to her, climbed up the bobstays and went on board."

The marines were suddenly impressed with a desire to go up and hear the band play.[19]

(At the siege of Newberne) Just before the battle began, a militia captain was endeavoring to get a company of Home Guards organized to go down to meet the invader. The men were on the ground, and the Captain wanted to form them into two ranks. But instead of the usual order, "In two ranks form company– march!" substituted one entirely original and shouted at the top of his voice, "In two lines right smart– go ahead!" [20]

(Lieutenant at Fort Lyon, Colorado, reprimands a corporal:) "Did I not tell you to put that light out?"

"Well," said Corporal W—, "I did." "You did. But why did you light it again?"

"Because you did not tell me to keep it out."

"You have been setting a bad example where you should have set a good one; you knew better than to do as you have done."

"I beg your pardon, Lieutenant; as I understand it, a soldier isn't supposed to know anything."[21]

(Private B— of the Regulars shot a crow belonging to General C—, who made him eat three or four mouthfuls before returning the Private's gun. With gun in hand, the Private made the General finish the crow.) The next day the General went to B's Colonel and complained that he had been grossly insulted by one of his soldiers the previous day.

The Colonel inquired which one. "Why," said the General, "he was a tall, lean, ill-favored fellow with red hair."

"Ha," said the Colonel, "I know him. He is always in some scrape. Orderly, bring B— here immediately. . . . B—, do you know this gentleman?"

"Yes, we are slightly acquainted," said B— (a happy thought striking him), "we dined together yesterday."[22]

(Correspondent at Murfreesboro writes:) Slick was passing General Johnson's headquarters one day, and without ceremony fired his gun almost in the face of the General himself. "What!" says the General, "Do you not know the penalty of firing your gun without orders to do so?"

"Why, no, sir," says Slick, very innocently.

"Well," replied the General, "I will tell you. It is the loss of a month's pay."

"You don't say so?" says Slick and very coolly puts his hand in his pocket and draws therefrom a greasy wallet, opens it, and offers the General thirteen dollars in greenbacks, saying, "Well, General, I guess I am able to stand the pressure!"[23]

(At recently captured Morris Island) a bronzed blue-

Harper's Monthly 1863

BUYING A SUBSTITUTE IN THE NORTH DURING THE WAR

jacket had just captured a mule and not without difficulty, mounted it, perching himself as near the animal's tail as there was a shadow of a chance– the mule objecting in every known way of a mule and in some ways until then unexhibited.

"Jack, sit more amidships," said Hardy, the First Engineer of the *Weehawken*, "and you'll ride easier."

"Captain," quoth old Salty, "this is the first craft that I was ever in command of, and it is a pity if I can't stay on the quarter-deck."[24]

When a mounted officer began licking his horse for shying at the bursting of a shell, General Lee called out, "Don't whip him, Captain, don't whip him. I've got just such an other foolish horse myself, and whipping does no good."[25]

(From Colonel Fremantle at Gettysburg:) When I got close up to General Longstreet, I saw one of his regiments advancing through the woods in good order; so, thinking I was just in time to see the attack, I remarked to the General that "I wouldn't have missed this for anything."

Longstreet was seated at the top of a snake fence at the edge of the wood, and looking perfectly calm and unperturbed. He replied laughing, "The devil you wouldn't! I would like to have missed it very much."[26]

A Western paper says that an Arkansas rebel cavalry colonel mounts his men by the following order: First Order: "Prepare fer ter git onter yer creeters." Second Order: "Git!"[27]

(An officer of the 16th United States Infantry writes from Galena, Illinois:) Eldest daughter Belle married last fall a chaplain in a rebel Tennessee regiment who, when the rebels evacuated Murfreesboro, went with his regiment, leaving his wife to return home. The father is a loyal man, but the rest of the family are badly secesh. The married daughter, during the spring and summer, was continually teasing her father to get her a military pass to go South to her husband, which he was not inclined to do. She got the pass, however, and commenced packing her things preparatory to leaving. About this time the news of the fall of Vicksburg came, and a horse, a very great favorite in the family, was taken violently sick and his life despaired of.

I was sitting one afternoon in the parlor, having a

Harper's Weekly
25 July 1863

The too Confiding South DRAFTING TERMS OF PEACE with the Federal Government.
(*See Richmond Papers, July 6, 7, 8.*)

social chat with the daughters, when the mother came in looking extremely dejected. "Ma," asked the youngest daughter, "what is the matter?"

"Oh dear, my daughter," she replied, at the same time straightening herself up in her chair in a peculiar manner. . . "Vicksburg has fallen, Belle is going down south, the horse is going to die, and the dear Lord only knows what will come upon us next!"[28]

Quartermasters in the army have a habit that, whenever the men surreptitiously confiscate a pig or a lamb, they seize on it and make use thereof at headquarters. The boys of the –th Indiana, in a recent case, were too fast for their Quartermaster. It happened on this wise: while out on picket they captured a nice young dog, dressed it neatly, and brought it into camp, taking care that Quartermaster should get wind of it. It was seized, and the headquarters ate, as they supposed, some nice fresh lamb. The joke was too good to keep, and the Quartermaster teased so unmercifully that a special order had to be issued to stop the fun.[29]

During the recent raid of John Morgan through this county, his men dropped a large number of worn-out horses. These were collected by the authorities and the best of them were distributed to those farmers whose horses had been stolen.

A few days afterward, a gentleman passing through the county was surprised to hear from a neighboring field the shrill sound of military commands: "Halt! File Left! Forward! March! Guide right!" He supposed that one of the numerous Home Guard companies to which the raid has given birth was going through the usual drill, but he discovered shortly that it was only a farmer plowing with one of Morgan's cast-off horses [30]

When General Lee repulsed Burnside at Fredericksburg with such terrible slaughter, the boys pitched in for booty, principally in the shape of boots. Nearly every man in Hays' brigade supplied himself from the battlefield. Shortly after, some shoes were being issued to the 7th Regiment. Colonel Penn (who knows every man in his command) saw Johnson coming up for a pair, and asked, "How does it happen, Johnson, that you did not get a pair

Harper's Weekly
22 August 1863

JEFF DAVIS'S LAST APPEAL TO ARMS.

" Fellow Citizens — the Victory is within your reach. You need but STRETCH FORTH
YOUR HANDS TO GRASP IT."—(*Address of Jeff Davis to his Soldiers.*)

48

from the field?"

"Well, Colonel, I couldn't make a raise."

"But all the rest of your company got boots."

"I know that, Colonel, but I was in bad luck. There *was* a wounded Yankee who had a pair on, just my fit, too; and I set up all night waiting for him to die. But he wouldn't." Johnson was allowed to draw.[31]

During the recent fight on the Rappahannock, General Early saw a man rushing past him. "Where are you going?"cried the General.

"To the rear," replied the man. "I am a noncombatant."

"Who are you?" demanded the General.

"I am a chaplain," replied the runner.

"Well," said the General, "here is consistency! For twenty years you have been wanting to get to heaven, and now that there is a chance, you run away from it!"[32]

A soldier of General Bragg's army was taken prisoner by the Yankees and escaped. He was called before General Bragg to give such information as he knew of the condition and intentions of the Yankee army. The following colloquy is said to have taken place:

General Bragg: "What is the Yankee General doing?"

Soldier: "Retreating."

General Bragg (incredulous): "Do you know what a retreat is?"

Soldier: "I ought to know, General. I have been with your army for nearly two years!"[33]

Our regiment was in Northern Mississippi and halting near a fine mansion. The boys were making for the chicken quarter, when the lady of the house appealed to the Colonel for protection, as she was "a good Union woman, and they all stood up for the Government!" Just then, one of the children cried out, "Oh, mother, that horrid Yankee's got Jeff Davis (a big rooster) and is going to wring his neck!" There was no further doubt about the loyalty of that household.[34]

One night, dark and rainy, Colonel S— and I were coming from Marietta to Camp Orchard, where the — Ohio Militia were encamped, being on the rampage after Morgan.

Harper's Weekly 8 August 1863

MR. LILLY LIVER as he appeared immediately after the publication of the General Order of the War Department for the arrest of all DESERTERS.

MR. LILLY LE VERE as he appeared in New York previous to the publication of the General Order of the War Department for the arrest of all DESERTERS.

We were riding at full gallop, and I told the Colonel that we had passed a sentry. He wheeled and returned to the sentinel, asking him why he did not order him to halt and give the word. The fellow was busy at something and cried out, "Hold on, till I load my gun!"[35]

While at Berryville, Virginia, we established our lines, and all persons residing within them and wishing to go beyond them were required to take the oath of allegiance. An intelligent contraband, wishing to go through, on learning the requirement, very innocently asked, "What is de oath?"

"You must swear to uphold the Constitution," replied the Marshal.

"Why," said Sam, "I can't hardly support the old woman, times is so dreadful hard!" The marshal let him pass.[36]

A correspondent from Chambersburg, Pennsylvania, informs us that when the rebel army was on the march from that place to Gettysburg, several privates stopped at the hotel of Mr. John Brown, in Fayetteville, and inquired for ale. The host informed them that he was just out of that article. One of the rebs remarked that they were going to Baltimore, and there they would get plenty. A few days after, when the rebs were retreating from Gettysburg, Brown happened to meet this same man on the South Mountain. He asked him if he had got any Baltimore ale. "No," replied Johnny Reb, "we only got as far as Gettysburg, where the Meade was too strong for us . . ."[37]

President Lincoln went with a young woman to a hospital in Washington, where she became much interested in the condition of a young man, and the following conversation ensued:

Lady: "Where were you wounded?"

Soldier: "At Antietam." Lady: "Yes, but *where* were you wounded?"

Soldier: "At Antietam."

Lady then begs the President to help her, as she feels a deep interest in the poor soldier.

President (taking the young lady by both hands affectionately): "My dear girl, the ball that hit him would have missed you."[38]

On his arrival at Pilot Knob, Missouri, as a prisoner, Confederate General Jeff Thompson had a long conversation with General Fisk, the commander at that post. Jeff swore on his honor that the Confederacy was a sure thing, bound to succeed, and all that.

"But confound those fellows in Southeast Missouri! When I was cavorting around Bird's Point two years ago, they were all friendly enough. But as I came through the country here as a prisoner, and told a few of them that I supposed they were right yet, hang me if they didn't have to stop and think which oath of allegiance they took last!"

The soldiers at Helena, in Arkansas, used to amuse the inhabitants of that place on their first arrival by telling them yarns, of which the following is a sample:

"Some time ago Jeff Davis got tired of the war and invited President Lincoln to meet him on neutral ground to discuss terms of peace. They met accordingly, and after a talk, concluded to settle the war by dividing the territory and stopping the fighting. The North took the Northern States, and the South the Gulf and seaboard Southern States. Lincoln took Texas and Missouri, and Davis Kentucky and Tennessee, so that all were parceled off excepting Arkansas. Neither would consent to take it. Lincoln didn't want it– Jeff wouldn't have it. And the war has been going on ever since.[39]

When the California Volunteers were busily engaged in building quarters near Salt Lake City last fall, a lieutenant of infantry had charge of working parties. One morning the sergeant of police failed to report the strength of his party by three men. The lieutenant demanded information and was informed that they could not be found. "Well," said the officer, "hunt them up, and when found send half of them to me and the other half to the stables."

"But, sir," replied the Sergeant, "there are only three missing." "Never mind that, Sergeant. You can not find them, send them all to the guardhouse."[40]

When Natchez was first occupied by the Feds, the business of daily passes was troublesomely great, so one of the officers of the Provost Marshal's office was sent out to ascertain who would do to trust with ten-day parole passes.

Among others, he found a very ladylike, pleasant mistress of a household, to whom he stated his business. The lady was very much obliged to him, but said she had that morning obtained a pass that would last her as long as there was any need for one. The officer did not think it possible; so she brought the pass and pointed out the words, "Good until retreat." The officer explained to her that "retreat" in that sense meant sunset as "reveille" meant daybreak. "Dear me!" said she folding up the short-lived pass, "I thought it meant until you retreated from Natchez!"[41]

An officer of the 25th Maine, observing a soldier belonging to a regiment camped nearby, industriously scratching himself, interrogated him thus: "What's the matter, my man– fleas?" "Fleas!" said he in a tone of unutterable scorn, "do you think I am a dog? No, sir, them is lice."[42]

Senator McDougall made a speech in the Senate against appointing of more generals. "Why," said he, referring to the preceding very stormy evening, "a man threw a stone at a dog last night and hit two brigadiers. And it wasn't a good night for stars, either."[43]

A captain of a steamboat on the Mississippi River, who had fought in the battles of the Texas Revolution, offered a free passage in his boat to any soldier who had participated in a certain engagement.
One day, a man claimed free passage, asserting that he was in the battle. He was referred to the Captain.
"In what capacity did you serve?"
"High private," was the reply.
"Stranger," said the Captain, "give me your hand. I have passed two thousand and eighty two who were in that fight, and you are the first private I have seen yet."[44]

Notes

[1] S. F. Martin to John P. Martin, 4 January, Missouri Historical Society, CWC Box 3.
[2] *Frank Leslie's Illustrated Weekly,* 28 February.
[3] *Harper's Monthly,* 26 February.
[4] *Mobile, Alabama, Record,* 24 February.

[5] *Frank Leslie's Illustrated Weekly*, 27 February.

[6] *Harper's Weekly*, 21 March.

[7] *Harper's Weekly*, 21 March.

[8] *Harper's Monthly*, March.

[9] *Ibid.*

[10] *Ibid.*, April.

[11] *Ibid.*, April

[12] *Army & Navy Messenger*, 1 May, 4.

[13] *Ibid.*, 27 June, 135

[14] *Ibid.*, 136.

[15] *Ibid.*, 137.

[16] *Ibid.*, 138-39.

[17] *Ibid.*, 139.

[18] *Ibid.*, July 282.

[19] *Ibid.*, September, 569-70.

[20] *Ibid.*, 570.

[21] *bid.*, 572.

[22] *Ibid.*

[23] *Ibid.*, 573.

[24] *Harper's Weekly,* 3 October, 631.

[25] (Richmond) *Record of News, History & Literature,* 8 October, 164.

[26] *Ibid.*

[27] *Frank Leslie's Weekly*, 31 October, 91.

[28] *Harper's Monthly*, October, 714.

[29] *Ibid., 716.*

[30] *Ibid.*

[31] (Richmond) *Southern Punch,* 24 October, 3.

[32] *Ibid*, 28 November, 6.

[33] *Ibid.*

[34] *Harpers Monthly*, November, 856.

[35] *Ibid.*

[36] *Ibid.*, 860.

[37] *Ibid.*

[38] S.L. Barlow to "Dear Joe" December 19, microfilm Vol. 8, Reel 8, Barlow Papers, Huntington Library.

[39] *Ibid.*, 137 .

[40] *Ibid.*, 140 .

[41] *Ibid.*, 140.

[42] *Old Abe's Joker, (*New York: Henry J. Wehman), 12.

[43] *Ibid.*, 18.

[44] *Ibid.*, 67.

1864

Sitting one day in a restaurant in Richmond, General Magruder had hardly tasted the merits of his repast when in sauntered a tall, long-haired, redshirted private in the First Louisiana, which regiment had just arrived in the city. With the utmost coolness, the redshirt sat himself down in the vacant chair opposite the General and let into the good things before him with a zest that plainly told of long marches and previous scanty rations. This was too much for the aristocratic old officer. Drawing himself up, and with one of his severest frowns and the harshest voice he could command, he exclaimed in tones of evident disgust, "Sir, what do you mean? Do you know at whose table you are sitting?"

The soldier, scarcely looking up, replied in the interval between a bite and a drink, "I know I am dreadful hungry, and I ain't a bit particular who I eat with since I've gone soldiering."[1]

General Benjamin McCulloch was very vain of his personal appearance and proud of his fame. About two days travel from Fort Smith in Arkansas a stranger rode up and inquired the winter way to Colonel Stone's winter quarters. The stranger was a perfect specimen of the genus butternut. He was dressed in bilious looking jeans, with a homemade hat and coarse boots, and wore his hair and beard very long. He was mounted on a good horse and carried on his shoulder a long, old-fashioned rifle. Before any of us had time to answer his inquiry, he cast his eyes on General McCulloch, and seemed to recognize him.

Dismounting at once, he advanced eagerly to the General with extended hand and a hearty, "Bless my soul, Joe! how do you do? What on earth are you doing here? The General saw the man was mistaken, but answered pleasantly and invited him to partake of our lunch, to which said lunch and demijohn the stranger did full and ample justice. He told the General (for to him he addressed all his conversation, as to an old friend) that he was a volunteer and had joined Colonel Stone's regiment of Texas Rangers, and that he intended to fight with "Old Ben McCulloch until we had gained our independence."

There was a young lass of Kentucky,
Who tho' little was loyal and plucky;
When her spark turned secesh
Though dear as her flesh,
She drummed him herself from Kentucky.

The New Book of Nonsense
1864

56

Old Ben enjoyed the man's mistake until we were about ready to start on, when he said to his Texas compatriot: "My friend, I reckon you are mistaken as to who you have been talking to. I don't think you know me, and perhaps have never seen me before."

"You be darned!" said Butternut. "I would know you, Joe, if I was to meet you in Africa!"

"Well now," said the General, getting tired of the new friend's familiarity, "Who do you take me for, anyway?"

"Take you for?" retorted Texas earnestly. "I don't take you for anybody. I know you to be Joe Baxter, what staid in the Perkins settlement in Collins County all last summer, a-sellin' chain-pumps and puttin' up lightnin'-rods!"[2]

The people of West Virginia have very queer ideas about our soldiers, and some of them were amusingly developed to the cavalrymen who made the recent raid on Wytheville. Among the officers was a certain Captain Y--, who has a remarkable fondness for buttermilk as a beverage, and who is in the habit of calling for it constantly at the farmhouses which he passes when on a scout. On the road to Wytheville he, with others, halted before a respectable-looking house, when they were met at the door by the frightened inmates with cries of, "The Yankees have come! The Yankees have come!" One of them, "a virgin on to forty," stretched forth her hands and with the most imploring gestures exclaimed, "Gentlemen, burn my house, destroy my property, do what you will– but spare my honor!"

"Confound your honor!" said the irate Captain Y–. "Have you got any buttermilk?"[3]

As the Army of the Mississippi under General Halleck was approaching Corinth on May 8, General Pope sent an orderly to inquire if General Palmer could hold his position.

"Tell General Pope that I can hold my position against the world, the flesh, and the devil!"

Before long, however, thm rebels– for they were over ten thousand strong– compelled the brigade to fall back upon the reinforcements which were ordered up.

The affair being over, General Palmer rode to the headquarters to report, and his appearance was the signal for a hearty laugh from the officers present. "How is it,

Palmer?" said General Pope, as he entered the tent.

"Well, General," said the gallant Palmer. "I can stand the world and the flesh, but the devil was too strong for me!"[4]

The following dialogue on sharpshooting is reported to have taken place between a Mississippi and a Yankee picket:

"I say, can you fellows shoot?"

"Wall, I reckon we can. Down in Mississippi we can knock a bumblebee off a thistle-blow at 300 yards."

"Oh, that ain't nothin' to the way we shoot up in old Vermont. I belonged to a military company ther, with a hundred men in the company, and we went out for practice every week. The cap'n draws us up in single file and sets a cider barrel rolling down the hill, and each man takes his shot at the bunghole as it turns up. It is afterwards examined, and if there is a shot that didn't go into the bunghole, the member who missed it is expelled. I belonged to the company ten years, and there hain't been anybody expelled yet."[5]

A letter from one of our officers at Point Isabel, Texas, among various anecdotes of our colored soldiers, relates: Some never had a dime in all their lives to call their own, and could not distinguish a one, two or five dollar greenback. One fellow paid ten dollars for a watch, and his lieutenant noticing it, inquired the time of day.

"Lor' Cap'n," replied the darkey (they call every officer "cap'n"), "I dunno. D'ye suppose I can tell?" "Why did you waste your money for a watch then?"

"Why, Cap'n, I bought it so dey couldn't keep dis chile on guard over two hours."[6]

Mrs. Partington says there must be a great many children killed on our battlefields, as there are always so many small arms found after a fight.[7]

What is a quartermaster? The man who gives the poor soldiers one quarter and keeps the rest himself.[8]

(An officer in the navy writes:) The other morning I was hurrying down to the wharf when I saw a drunken sailor trying to induce a shore-boatman to take him off.

"Have you any money?" said the wily boatman.

"Money– money, you fool! . . . If I had any money, what the deuce would I be going aboard ship for?"[9]

An officer charged with the work complained to Colonel –- that it was impossible to construct the battery on account of the depth of the mud. "But it must be done," was the answer. "Make requisition for anything you want in the wy of force and material, but the work must be done!"

The subordinate retired and sent in a requisition for what he thought necessary, and among the items was one for "twenty-five men, twenty feet long, to work in mud eighteen feet deep!"[10]

(A Nebraska correspondent writes about raw troops assigned to guard bridges on Iron Mountain and St. Louis Railroad:) Our captain, a large, corpulent man, was also raw. He paraded the company and proceeded to invent a series of tactics of his own, beginning with, "Now, boys, the first thing to be did is to shoulder arms, and you must know beforehand what the order means. 'Shoul' means grab your gun with your left hand; 'der' means 'up'; and 'arms' means to put our left arm by your side, quick."

"The next thing to be did is to 'order arms.' 'Or' means take hold of your gun with your left hand; 'der' means down; and - -"

"Hold on, Cap," said one of the boys. "You said just a moment ago that 'der' meant up." The Captain turned red, white, and blue by turns, and at length broke out with, "Sergeant P–-, take that man to the guardhouse and keep him there," adding, "what does he know about soldiers?"[11]

A soldier in one of the Kentucky camps, during one of the cold nights, says the motto with them is, "United we sleep; divided we freeze."

(Bread is scarce in the South, as witness this dialogue:)

"Who's there?"

"Baker."

What do you want?"

To leave your bread."

"Well, you needn't make such a fuss about it– put

There was an old lady of Norfolk, who always was saying before folk,
I to a mean yankee will never say "thankee," this civil old lady of Norfolk.

The New Book of Nonsense
1864

it through the keyhole."[12]

An officer of the regular army, Lieutenant Manus of the Tenth Infantry, recently met a sad rebuff at Fort Kearney, Nebraska Territory. The Lieutenant was promenading in full uniform one day and approaching a sentinel (volunteer) was challenged with, "Halt! who comes there?" The Lieutenant, with contempt in every lineament of his face, expressed his ire with an indignant– "Ass!" The sentry's reply, apt and quick, came, "Advance, Ass, and give the countersign!"[13]

A clergyman, happening to pass a boy weeping bitterly, halted and asked, "What is the matter, my little fellow?" The boy replied–"Before, we could hardly get enough to eat of anything, and now what shall we do, for there's another one come?"

"Hush thy complaining and wipe off those tears," said the clergyman, "and remember that He never sends mouths without he sends victuals to put in them."

"I know that,"said the boy, "but then He sends all the mouths to our house and all the victuals to your house."[14]

A young minister, in a highly elaborate sermon which he preached, said several times when giving some new exposition on a passage, "The critics and commentators do not agree with me here." Next morning a poor woman came to see him with something in her apron. She said her husband heard his sermon and thought it was a very fine one; and as he said, "The common taters did not agree with him," he had sent some of the very best Jersey blues.[15]

(A Vicksburg correspondent reports:) During the siege of Corinth it became necessary to go some ten miles over the worst of roads to Pittsburg Landing to draw forage and provisions, and many were the expedients resorted to by the boys to escape the hard task. One morning at roll-call our lieutenant said, "Any of the boys who would like a drill, step to the front." Not many came forward. "Now, you rear rank men, each take a horse, go to the Landing, and bring back a sack of oats."[16]

A committee, just previous to the fall of Vicksburg, solicitous for the morale of our armies, took it upon them selves to visit the President and urge removal of General Grant.

"What for?" asked Uncle Abe.

"Why," replied the busy-bodies, "he drinks too much whisky."

"Ah!" rejoined Uncle Abe, "can you inform me, gentlemen, where General Grant procures his whisky?"

The committee confessed they could not. "Because," added Uncle Abe, with a merry twinkle in his eye, "if I find out, I'll send a barrel of it to every general in the field."[17]

Yesterday a Western correspondent, in search of something definite in relation to the fighting now going on, stepped into the White House and asked the President if he had anything authentic from General Grant. The President stated that he had not, as Grant was like the man that climbed the pole and then pulled the pole up after him.[18]

(A correspondent from Huntsville, Alabama writes:) On the morning before the battle (for Mission Ridge, near Chattanooga) the troops were drawn up in battle order and stood till near noon. As the weather was quite cold, the General, in riding along the lines, saw them shivering, especially those thinly clad. "Poor fellows!" said he, "Poor fellows! Got no overcoats. Too lazy to carry them."[19]

While I was on picket the other day, an intelligent contraband, passing towards Portsmouth, was asked by one of our guards if she had a pass. "No, Sah," she replied, "but I'se got de smallpox." She was allowed to pass.[20]

(A lady in Missouri contributes:) During the siege of Vicksburg some of the Sixth Missouri cavalry visited the former residence of "President Davis," and found the blacks all very much alarmed at the near approach of General Grant, whom they believed would immediately devour them. The frightened creatures asked numberless questions of the boys as to what they should do to appease him if he should visit them. The boys told them the General was not very frightful, and if they would assemble in the yard on his approach and give him three cheers they would be safe. They were very much amused on returning to find the darkeys had nicely swept a place under the trees in the yard and had set out three of the best chairs the mansion afforded.[21]

In the summer of '62 the Twelfth Massachusetts Volunteers were in General Abercromby's brigade. On the march from Winchester to Warrington they sorely tried the General's patience by straggling and foraging on their own hook, often-times getting miles ahead of the marching column.

One day the General, finding himself some few miles ahead of his column, entered a house on the roadside to get a hasty breakfast. Scarcely had he been seated when he saw half a dozen soldiers pass by toward the front. He halted them at once with the interrogatory, "What regiment do you belong to?"

"Twelfth Massachusetts," was the answer.

"The Twelfth? Ha! I know you boys. You're always ahead of me. Go back to your regiment. I intend to lead the brigade myself this morning!" [22]

"A day or two ago I went to Marietty after forage and got back yesterday, and the Women and Children were coming back into town by the Hundred. They were more scared than hurt. The rebs say that Captain (General) Hooker dont fight fa(i)r, for regiment dont come rot up squar and fight 'em but weuns go way arround and shoot 'em endways, then they say they have to fall back."[23]

While we were foraging in Sequatchie, the campaign which ended with the battle of Chickamauga, our boys used to get up cotillion parties, etc. in the country, which were well attended by the ladies, both Union and Secesh, of the valley. The latter were very careful on such occasions about the language they used in the presence of the boys, lest they might offend them. One of the ladies stepped up to Wash, the fiddler, and said very politely, "Will you be so kind as to play the *Federal Doodle*?"[24]

After Lee recrossed the Potomac last summer, our regiment had a sharp fight with Stuart's cavalry at Shepherdstown, Virginia. Most of our men were dismounted and fighting under the cover of trees and inequalities of the ground.

Harper's Weekly 11 June 1864

GRANT TURNING LEE'S FLANK.

One of the boys from Company, a fellow full of jest as he was of life, exclaimed to his comrades, "Do you see that tall, lank-looking reb with a straw hat off? Now keep your eye on him, and see him jump." He fired and, as the smoke arose, he leaped into the air exclaiming, "By thunder, the wrong boy jumped!"[25]

> From *Life In The Confederate Army:*
> "Five days of the year we have fasting and prayer;
> For the rest of the time, we fight, drink, and swear".[26]

A Canadian newspaper, referring to the influx of sneaks from the States who flock into Canada to escape the draft, says: "They are coming, Father Abraham, 500,000 more; but, unfortunately for you and for us they are coming the wrong way."[27]

The 49th Ohio National Guard, commanded by Colonel DeWolf, was ordered to report at Johnson's Island. One of the companies, upon disembarking, was ordered to fall in and march off by their captain, who did not know a single command, in this wise: "Choose partners, gentlemen, get in two rows, and march endways, as you did yesterday."[28]

(A Georgia correspondent writes:) One night General –- was out on the line, and observed a light on the mountain opposite. Thinking it was a signal light of the enemy, he remarked to his artillery officer that a hole could easily be put through it. Whereupon the officer turning to the corporal in charge of the gun, said: "Corporal, do you see that light?"

"Yes, Sir."

"Put a hole through it."

The Corporal sighted the gun and when all was ready, he looked up and said, "Captain, that's the moon."

"Don't care for that," was the Captain's ready response, "put a hole through it anyhow."[29]

(Another Georgia correspondent says:) A deserter had come into our lines a few days ago and was passing to the rear when one of our fellows hailed him with, "Hello, Johnny, where are you going now?"

"Well, General Hardee made a speech the other day

and told us to 'strike for our homes and firesides,' and as I live in Tennessee, I concluded to strike for mine!"[30]

"I say, Yank, what's the matter on your side of the tree?"

The Yank immediately replied that he wanted to go for water.

"Well, go ahead," answered Johnny, "I'll watch both sides till you come back."[31]

When Prince Napoleon visited our army at Manassas, his supper the first night was half-picked bone – provisions being so scarce and the fare of our generals so scanty that nothing better could be provided from the vicinity. The next day he rode over the battlefield, but turned very sick at the sight and odor that met his senses. Subsequently he reviewed our troops. While riding down the line, he expressed a desire to pass back in the rear.

Lieutenant Colonel Skinner of the 1st Virginia Regiment, who was by the side of the Prince, for the moment was placed in a dilemma, but recovering himself quickly, a flush mantled his rugged face, as he replied in French: "Your royal highness, we would gladly take you to the rear, but the fact is, the linen of the men is in rather an exposed condition. It being a part of the person which we never expect to show to the enemy, our men think rags there of but little consequence."[32]

While the Yankees were occupying Canton, Mississippi, a little boy, five years of age, passing by a bevy of soldiers, shouted, "Hurrah for Jeff Davis!"

"Hurrah for the devil!" was the indignant response.

"That's right," said the little fellow, "you hurrah for your captain, and I'll hurrah for mine."[33]

At the battle of Kingston, when the shells were exploding around the battery of artillery, a chaplain asked one of the soldiers sitting on his horse, whether he was supported by Divine Providence. The soldier replied, "No, he was supported by the 9th New Jersey."[34]

When our army entered Chambersburg, Pennsylvania, some of the Union females of the town, relying on their sex and the gallantry of the "rebels" for protection, jawed the troops from windows and doors as they passed by. There was one of those women whose tongues, we suppose, could not do justice to the occasion, who flourished from her bosom a small Union flag and who, standing in a door, made all manner of ugly faces at our soldiers as they marched along. But her ladyship caught a tartar in making a mouth at a tall, ragged rebel in the ranks who, fixing his eye in disdain on the flag that waved from aimed, "Madam, you had better tear that thing from your bosom– we rebels are hell on breastworks!"[35]

In the capitol square in Richmond, a drunken soldier accosted the President: "Are you Mr. Davis?"
"I am," was the stern reply.
"Are you President of the Confederate States?"
"I am."
"Well, I thought you looked like a postage stamp." [36]

Among other incidents of the battle of Murfreesboro, we heard of one in which a soldier observed a rabbit lopping across the field under a heavy fire. "Run, cottontail," he said; "if I hadn't a reputation to sustain, I'd travel, too!"[37]

A correspondent of the Eutaw *Whig and Observer* wrote thus from Fredericksburg:
A young, stout, hale, hearty man in a South Carolina regiment went to General Lee for the purpose of getting a furlough, when the following amusing incident took place–
General Lee: Sir, do you know the position of a soldier?
Soldier (saluting the General): I do, Sir.
General Lee: Assume the position of a soldier. I want to see if you can execute two or three orders as I give them.
General Lee (viewing him closely and scrutinizing his position) About face, forward march (and never said "halt").[38]

A lady went to General Milroy and asked for a pass to go over the lines. He said, "I will give you a pass to hell."
She told him she did not know his lines extended that far. She had often heard it, but now had it from his own lips.[39]

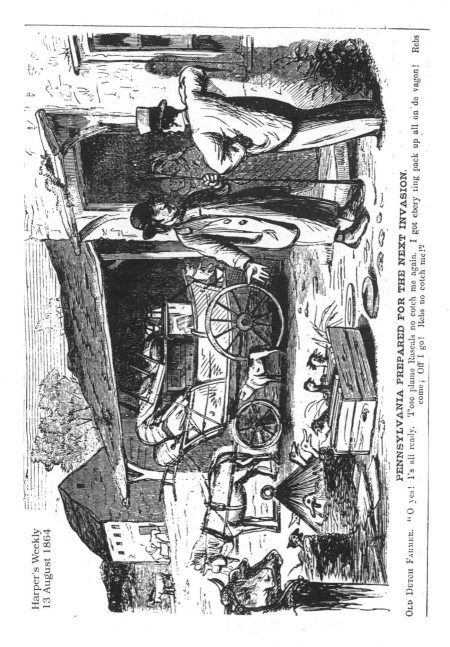

Harper's Weekly
13 August 1864

PENNSYLVANIA PREPARED FOR THE NEXT INVASION.

Old Dutch Farmer. "O yes! I's all ready. Tose plaue Rascals no cotch me again. I got ebery ting pack up all on 'de vagon! Rebs come; Off I go! Rebs no cotch me!?"

"Hermes," the correspondent of the Charleston, South Carolina *Mercury,* related the following incident: At Sharpsburg, General Lee, meeting one of the many stragglers, inquired, "Where are you going, Sir?"

"Going to the rear."

"What are you going to the rear for?"

"Well, I've been stung by a bung, and I'm what they call demoralized."

This was enough. General Lee hadn't the heart to say more to an innocent who had been stung by a bung– meaning, probably, that he had been stunned by a bomb.[40]

Sometimes a rousing cheer is heard in the distance. It is explained (by the *Richmond Whig*): "Boys, look out! – here comes Old Stonewall or an old hare, one or t'other"– they being the only individuals who invariably bring down the house.[41]

(Quoting the Chattanooga, Tennessee *Rebel*:) "Those people who have a great deal to say about being ready to shed their last drop of blood are amazin' particular about the first drop."[42]

The Yankees are determined to have their fun, if their leaders are afraid to fight. On the First of April 1863, between four thousand and five thousand of them landed near Pocotaligo, South Carolina, and with an air of boldness that augured something terrible, took up the line of march inland.

General Evans, hearing of the movement, immediately dispatched four regiments to engage them and dispute their passage. On coming in sight, the Yankees were found in full retreat to their boats, but a tall pole had been stuck in the ground at the turning point, and on it inscribed, in large letters, "April Fool!"[43]

(Talking to Stonewall Jackson's old body servant) someone asked him how he came to be so much in the confidence of his master. "Lord, Sir," said he, "massa never tells me nothing, but the way I knows is this: massa says his prayers twice a day, morning and night – but if he gets out of bed two or three times in the night to pray, you see I just commences packing my haversack, for I knows there will be

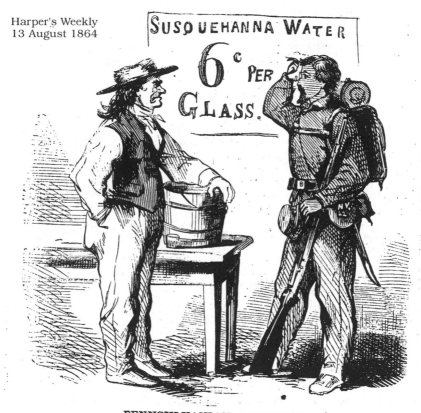

Harper's Weekly
13 August 1864

SUSQUEHANNA WATER
6ᶜ PER GLASS.

PENNSYLVANIAN GRATITUDE.

ABLE-BODIED PENNSYLVANIAN, "Six cents a glass rayther dear, you think? Pshaw! what's the good of having you fellows here from New York, if we can't make something out of you to cover what we lose by the rebel raiders?"

the devil to pay next day."[44]

(The *Cincinnati Enquirer* reportedly said:) A republican gentleman of this city, in a recent visit to Washington, called on President Lincoln. In the course of the conversation, the visitor inquired if his excellency had not felt some alarm about the safety of the capitol, to which the President gave the following classic reply: "O, the Cabinet were somewhat alarmed, but I wasn't skeer'd a hooter."[45]

A Western paper relates the following exemption story:

"Doctor, if the lame foot won't answer, I have another all-sufficient reason – one that you cannot refuse me exemption for."

"What is it?"

"Why, the fact is, Doctor, I have not good sense. I am an idiot."

"Ah!" said the Doctor, "what proof have you of that?"

"Proof conclusive," said the applicant. "Why, sir, I voted for Jim Buchanan, and if that isn't proof of a man's being a damned idiot, I don't know how idiocy could be proven."[46]

A captain of Munford's cavalry (2nd Virginia) on picket after the battle of Fredericksburg, was accosted by the Yankee picket opposite to him with the query: "Have you a sorry corporal with you?"

"No," answered the Captain, "but what do you want with him?"

"We want to trade you Burnside for him."[47]

A Yankee puffer having stated that Hooker's headquarters are in the saddle, the Mobile Advertiser observes. "To think of a general that didn't know his hindquarters from his headquarters expecting to whip General Lee."[48]

A little boy in Nashville, Tennessee, a vender of pie, started out with his basket when he was accosted by a federal on a horse. A tempting pie was purchased, when the Federal, suspicious by a depraved nature, requested the boy to taste a piece. The boy complied, returned it, and the federal commenced eating the pie, understanding the fears

Harper's Weekly
17 September
1864

of Uncle Sam's hireling, immediately sang out. "Don't you think I know'd which side had the p'isin'?" The pie was thrown down hastily, but the boy kept the dime and the joke.[49]

About the beginning of the war, General Hardee was forming the nucleus of an army in southeast Missouri, and being a great disciplinarian, was very active in teaching his men the rules and duties of a soldier's life. It happened one night that a sentinel had been placed to guard some stores near the entrance of the General's headquarters. Returning home rather late from a tour of inspection, he passed the sentinel a few paces from his door, and not being honored with the usual salute of "present arms," he halted and in a kind but commanding tone said, "Don't you know me?"

"No, Sir," replied the uncouth Arkansian. "Who are you?"

"I am General Hardee, Sir!"

Whereupon the raw recruit advanced a few paces, put out his hands for a sake, and said in a most familiar tone, "My name is Bill Dickerson, and I'm right glad to make your acquaintance!"[50]

At the siege of Lexington, Missouri, an old Texan, dressed in buckskin and armed with a long rifle, used to go up to the works every morning about seven o'clock, carrying his dinner in a tin pail. Taking a good position, he banged away at the Federals till noon, then in an hour ate his dinner, after which he resumed operations till six p.m., when he returned home to supper and a night's sleep. The next day, a little before seven, saw him, dinner and rifle in hand, trudging up street to begin again his regular day's work, and in this style he continued till the surrender.[51]

In one of our Southern cities, a new commandant having been there assigned to duty, applied in person at the residence of a Mrs. Measle, one of the handsomest mansions in the town, with the following mandate: "Madam, I am Brigadier-General Joseph D. Wilkinson, commander of this District."

"I am Mrs. Elizabeth Measle. You can't get it! Good morning."[52]

Since the late order promulgated by the General allowing brief furloughs to two enlisted men and one commissioned officer from each company in the service, a captain in the 28th Georgia Regiment made application for one of the leaves for a member of his company, then in the regimental band. The document went "approved and respectfully forwarded" through the offices of colonel, brigadier general, etc. to General D.H. Hill, who most unmercifully left the applicant without hope by the final endorsement thereon: "Shooters furloughed before tooters!"[53]

Wendell Phillips put up at a hotel in Charleston, South Carolina, had breakfast served in his room, and was waited on by a slave. The negro seemed more anxious about the breakfast than he was about his relations and the condition of his soul, and finally in despair Mr. Phillips ordered him to go away, saying that he couldn't bear to be waited on by a slave.

"Excuse me, massa," said the negro, "must stay here, 'cause I am responsible for the silverware."[54]

Abe, once reminded of the enormous cost of the war, remarked, "Ah, yes! that reminds me of a wooden-legged amateur who happened to be with a Virginia skirmishing party when a shell burst near him, smashing his artificial limb to bits and sending a piece of iron through the calf of a soldier near him. The soldier grinned and bore it like a man, while the amateur was loud and emphatic in his lamentation. Being rebuked by the wounded soldier, he replied, "Oh, yes, it's all well enough for it. Your leg didn't cost you anything and will heal up, but I paid two hundred dollars for mine.[55]

Notes

[1] *Harper's Monthly,* January, 283.
[2] *Ibid.*
[3] *Ibid.,* 283-84.
[4] *Harper's Monthly,* February,427.
[5] *(Rendezvous of Distribution, VA.)Soldiers' Journal,* 2 March, 23.
[6] *Ibid.,* 16 March, 39.
[7] *Southern Punch,* 19 March, 7.

[8] *Ibid.,* 26 March, 4.

[9] *Harper's Monthly,* March, 567-68.

[10] *Ibid.,* 570.

[11] *Ibid.,* 571.

[12] *Harpers Weekly,* 16 April, 250.

[13] *Harpers Monthly,* April, 716.

[14] *Black Warrior,* 19 May, 4.

[15] *Ibid.*

[16] *Harper's Monthly,* May, 856.

[17] *Lincolniana* (New York: J. F. Feeks, 1864), 61.

[18] *Washington Union,* 16 May.

[19] *Harper's Monthly,* May, 859.

[20] *Ibid.,* 857.

[21] *Ibid.,* June, 139.

[22] *Ibid.,* 137.

[23] Unpublished letter of Delos W. Lake, Headquarters, Company E, I9th Michigan Infantry to "Mother Arnold," 11 July 1864; Huntington Library accession number LK 55; courtesy Charles Royster.

[24] *Harper's Monthly,* July, 269.

[25] *Ibid.,* 274.

[26] *Harper's Weekly,* 6 August, 507.

[27] (Philadelphia) *Campaign Dial,* 8 September.

[28] *Harper's Monthly,* September.

[29] *Ibid.,* October, 684.

[30] *Ibid.,* November, 816.

[31] *Ibid.,* 819.

[32] Felix De Fontaine, *Marginalia* (Columbia, South Carolina: Privately Printed, 1864), 6-7.

[33] *Ibid.,* 17.

[34] *Ibid.,* 51.

[35] *Ibid.,* 67.

[36] *Ibid.,* 79.

[37] *Ibid.,* 79.

[38] *Ibid.,* 81.

[39] *Ibid.,* 90.

[40] *Ibid.,* 94.

[41] *Ibid.,* 108.

[42] *Ibid.,* 105.

[43] *Ibid.,* 116.

[44] *Ibid.,* 145.

[45] *Ibid.,* 143.

[46] *Ibid.,* 158.

[47] *Ibid.,* 159.
[48] *Ibid.,* 191.
[49] *Ibid.,* 192.
[50] *Ibid.,* 195.
[51] *Ibid.,* 200.
[52] *Ibid.,* 209.
[53] *Ibid.,* 210.
[54] *Ibid.,* 216.
[55] *Old Abe's Jokes,* 42.

1865

A contraband who came into Sheridan's lines, when questioned about the rebels arming the colored men, said, "About half de colored men think dey would run directly over to de Yankees wid de arms in their hands, and toder half think dey would jiss stand and fire a few volleys to the rear fust, 'fore de run—dat's all de difference. [1]

Colt's arms are useful when you want to fight, but if you want to run away, colt's legs are better.[2]

As the surgeon was going his rounds (in an open field hospital, Locust Grove, after the battle of the Wilderness), examining patients he came to a sergeant of a New York regiment, who had been struck by a bullet in the left breast, right over the region of the heart. The doctor, surprised at the narrow escape of the man, ejaculated, "Why, my man, where in the name of goodness could your heart have been?"
The poor fellow, with a faint and sickly smile, replied, "I guess it must have been in my mouth just then, Doctor."[3]

(After the battle of the Wilderness) we were talking on indifferent subjects when a young man (now dead, poor boy!) spoke up. He told us how he had lain all night upon the battlefield, and in spite of the pain from his shattered limb and the usual dreadful cries round him, he felt much inclined to sleep. This was rendered impossible by an old owl that had perched itself – a fitting serenader on the bloody field – over his head. He said that the confounded thing kept crying, "Who– who hit yer? Who– who hit yer?"

(Serving with) the Federal forces under Major General A.J. Smith at Holly Springs, Mississippi, in August 1864, Colonel A–– wrote in the album of Miss Clemmie who'd lost ten beaus to Yankee bullets:

'Tis certain, Miss Clemmie, whether Fed or Confed,
In the plain course of nature you're destined to wed;
Some Lord of Creation will lovingly kneel,
And pour forth his tender and fervent appeal,
If the Feds and Confeds will cease this vain strife,

A MAN KNOWS A MAN.

"Give me your hand, Comrade! We have each lost a LEG for the good cause; but, thank GOD, we never lost HEART."

And leave a man living to make you his wife. [4]

During the summer the Virginia farmers, being much troubled by our boys foraging, were apt to conceal their stock and poultry as much as possible. One of the boys exclaimed, upon returning to camp without any spoils, "There is nothing on the whole plantation but a yoke of oxen, and they were chained to the bed post in the house!"[5]

A feminine rebel, a Memphian and a widow, who shall go by the name of Mrs. C—, was recently going up the river on one of the Cairo packets, when she got into an excited discussion with Colonel B—, on the subject of the war. It took place in the ladies' cabin and soon brought around them a crowd of eager listeners. She poured whole broadsides of sarcasm into the Colonel, who received them with his characteristic good humor. The closing scene of the discussion is given by my informant as follows:
"You may overrun the whole South," said Mrs C—. "You may burn our towns, lay waste our plantations, maim or kill the last man, but then, Sir, we will arm our boys with squirrel rifles and shotguns and put one behind every stump in the land. What will you do then?"
"O," replied the Colonel, "we will be compelled to surround the stumps."
"But when you have accomplished that, we the women of the South will bare our breasts to the Federal bayonets."
"You dare not do that, madam."
"Why not, Sir?"
"For the simple reason, madam, it is unlawful. Your Confederate Congress has made it criminal for you to expose your cotton to the Yankee forces."[6]

During the siege of Mobile all the ladies were hard at work at one time making bags to be filled with sand. Sewing circles, churches, and schools all lent a willing hand. One school for young ladies sent it's share with patriotic mottoes. One zealous young lady's name can now be seen as follows: "God save the South for Mary Brown!"[7]

An unsophisticated countryman the other day com-

Harper's Weekly 15 April 1865

FROM OUR SPECIAL WAR CORRESPONDENT.

"CITY POINT, VA., *April* —, 8.30 A.M.
"All seems well with us."—A. LINCOLN.

ing into Richmond with a load of wood saw a military officer, followed at a respectable distance by two orderlies– all three mounted and in full gallop. "Good gracious," said he, "haven't they caught him yet? I was in about three weeks ago, and they were a-runnin' him then."[8]

The only joke we ever heard of being perpetrated by General Sherman is the following: As he rode into the city of Raleigh, the capital of North Carolina, he overtook a regiment of veterans tramping past the State House, many of whom were singing snatches of various favorite songs. For a few moments Sherman listened and then called out, "Well, boys, that's good enough, but I'll tell you what I would sing . . . 'Raleigh round the flag, boys!'"[9]

About seven miles from Richmond, I saw a man lying under the shade of a tree assiduously chewing tobacco. After saluting him and asking several questions, to which I received lazy Yesses and noes, I asked him to what churches the people in that neighborhood usually went. "Well, not much to any."

"What are their religious views?"

"Well, not much of any."

"Well, my friend, what are your religious views?" I asked.

The man answered slowly and sleepily, "My own 'pinion is, that them as made me'll take care of me."[10]

O'Toole is a teamster in Captain McKorkey's celebrated battery which contributed so materially to our success at Antietam, and, in fact, saved the day. One day during the prevailing season of mud, as Lieutenant Colonel Bernstein was riding a tour of inspection, he met the jovial teamster wending his way towards the battery stable with a large shovel over his shoulder.

"Where are you going, my brave lad?" said the Colonel, who always has a kind word for our gallant boys.

"To curry the ears of me mool."

"Why do you groom only the ears of your mule?"

"Shure, thim's all ov 'im remains out o' the mud, Sur!"[11]

In Mississippi a rebel was caught who was accused

ABOUT THE SIZE OF IT.

Uncle Sam. "Stand clear there, all airth and ocean! My hands are free now, and I'm goin' to hyst a flag so big that it'll cover most o' the land and a good bit o' the sea!"

of being a spy. As usual in such cases, there was strong talk of hanging. Before starting on the march next morning the question arose, what had been done with the spy? "They hung him at daybreak this morning," says someone confidently.

"No, they didn't," said our orderly sergeant drily; "he had a sore throat, and they excused him!"[12]

One of the provost guards brought a man into the office charged with stealing watermelons. The charge was proved, and I sentenced him to ten days in the provost guardhouse. As he was being led away, I said to him, "I hope, Tom, I shall never see you here again."

He turned to me with a peculiarly shrewd expression and said, "You wouldn't have seen me this time, Cap'n, if the soldiers hadn't caught me."[13]

When General Sully last summer, on his expedition to the Devil's Lake, passed Fort Berthscol, quite a number of Indians had gathered there to see him and make peace. They complained a good deal of the dry weather and wished the General would make rain the same as Father de Smet, the missionary that used to see them, had done. The General promised them he would do the best he could. It happened that shortly afterward a heavy thundershower passed, flooding everything. The Indians were greatly pleased and called the General a great medicine man. But they said it was a little too much at once. "Well," said the General, "I know it, but I couldn't stop the thing after it started."[14]

A woman living near Atlanta, before we took it, had a handsome daughter of sweet sixteen, whom we often heard saying: "Oh, ma, when *are* the Yankees coming to ravish us all? We hear of their coming nearer every day, and all of us girls are waiting impatiently to know all about it, and find out if the Yankees really will do as much badness to us as people say they will."[15]

A member of one of the (Mississippi) volunteer companies which went down to Pensacola, being accustomed to fresh water, living in the interior, and not having been on the Gulf of Mexico before, he was in blissful ignorance of its briny properties. Getting up in the morning to perform his daily ablutions, he drew a bucketful of water, set it down near some of his comrades, and retired for soap and towel. The consequences can be imagined. Recovering from the shock, and rubbing his burning eyeballs, he exclaimed, "I can whip the damned rascal that salted this water! A man can't draw a bucket of water and leave it for a few minutes without some prank is played on him."[16]

One day a wealthy old lady, whose plantation was in the vicinity of the camp, came in and inquired for General (O.H.) Payne. When the commander made his appearance, the old lady in warm language told him that his men had stolen her last coop of chickens, and demanded restoration or its value in money.

"I am sorry for you, Madam," replied the General, "but I can't help it. The fact is, Madam, we are determined to squelch out the rebellion, if it cost every damned chicken in Tennessee."[17]

Prisoners captured at Cheraw said it was no use fighting Sherman, for if the devil had him in hell, he would flank him and get to heaven.[18]

It was grotesque, too, the humor they had, even when most afflicted. I remember well, one poor fellow lying, with a shattered arm, upon the operating table at Fairfax Court House while some two or three surgeons were hurriedly consulting, or disputing, whether the arm should be taken off close to the shoulder, or down near the elbow:– "Long life to you, gentlemen," said the sufferer with a brogue, "and leave me enough to hug my girl with!"[19]

During a stagecoach ride in the Southwest (naval officer R--, an inveterate cigar smoker), his stock of Havanas reduced to two, "Only two cigars left (he said). Well, I must fully enjoy them!" (The stage takes on a lady passenger:) "Madam, do you object to a cigar?"

To which she readily replied, much to his surprise and consternation, "Well, Mister, I don't care if I do take one, if you've got some handy. I left my pipe to home."[20]

Notes

1 *Soldier's Friend,* March, 4.
2 *Ibid.*
3 *Harper's Monthly,* March, 541.
4 *Ibid.,* 539.
5 *Ibid,* 543.
6 *[Boston] Gleason's Pictorial Dollar Weekly,* 27 May, 327.
7 *Harper's Monthly,* July, 269.
8 *(Philadelphia) Soldier's Casket,* July, 449.
9 *Ibid,* 450.
10 *The Soldier's Friend* , August, 4.
11 *Harper's Monthly,* August, 408.
12 *Ibid,* November, 812.
13 *Ibid,* 814.
14 *Ibid., 816.*
15 *Hairbreadth Escapes,* (Cincinnati: P. C. Brown, 1865), 149.
16 Charles S. Greene, *Thrilling Stories,* (Philadelphia: J. E. Potter, 1866), 364-65.
17 *A Legacy of Fun* (London: Frederick Fourah, 1865), 5.
18 George C. Lawson, 45th Illinois Volunteers, *Sherman's Campaign* (Broadside 307002, Huntington Library Manuscript collection).
19 Greene, *Thrilling Stories*, 364-65.
20 *Harper's Monthly,* December, 134.

At a council of generals early in the war, one remarked that Major —- was wounded and would not be able to perform a duty that it was proposed to assign him. "Wounded!" said Jackson, "If it is really so, I think it must have been an accidental discharge of his duty."[1]

"Joe," said a soldier to a comrade who was reading the morning paper, "where the devil's Status Quo? I see this paper says our army's in Status Quo."
"Dunno!" replied Joe– "reckon she must be the east fork of the Chickamorgy."

A lieutenant was promenading in full uniform one day and approaching a volunteer on sentry, who challenged him with, "Halt! Who comes there?" The lieutenant, with contempt in every lineament of his face, expressed his ire with an indignant, "Ass!" The sentry's reply, apt and quick, came, "Advance, ass, and give the countersign."[2]

Army teamsters are proverbial for the scientific volubility with which they swear. A teamster with the Cumberland army got stuck in the mud, and he let fly a stream of profane epithets that would have astonished "our army in Flanders," even. A chaplain passing at the time was greatly shocked. "My friend," said he to the teamster, "do you know who died for sinners?"
"Damn your conundrums. Don't you see I'm stuck in the mud?"[3]

We have had a box-and-a-half of shoeblacking given to each man. You will remember that in my last letter I stated that G.F., one of the privates, had no shoes. When the Colonel gave us the blacking he said he wanted us to look as much alike as possible. So G.F. went to work and blacked his feet and polished them, and when the Colonel came along on dress parade, he asked G.F. why he did that. He replied, "To look as much alike as possible." – The Colonel burst out laughing and went, after parade, to the store and bought him a pair of shoes with his own money.[4]

A soldier of Bates' division of the Confederate army, after the command had run two days from Nashville, had thrown away his gun and accouterments and, alone in the woods, sat down and commenced thinking – The first chance he had for such a thing. Rolling up his sleeves and looking at his legs and general physique, he thus gave vent to his feelings: "I am whipped, badly whipped, and somewhat demoralized, but no man can say I am scattered."[5]

One of the farmers in the vicinity of Culpepper, whose possessions lay in a district where both armies foraged, the old chap, one day, while surveying ruefully the streaks in the soil where his fences once stood, remarked with much feeling: "I hain't took no sides in this yer rebellion, but I'll be doggorned if both sides hain't took me!"[6]

During the march of McClellan's army up the Peninsula from Yorktown, a tall Vermont soldier got separated from his regiment and was trudging along through the mud, endeavoring to overtake it. Finally coming to a crossing, he was puzzled as to which road he should take. But on seeing one of the natives, his countenance lighted up at the prospect of obtaining the desired information, and he inquired, "Where does this road lead to?"
"To hell!" was the surly answer of the native.
"Well," drawled the Vermonter, "judging by the lay of the land, and the appearance of the inhabitants, I kalkerlate I'm 'most thar."[7]

It was a warm, pleasant day. We (of the 41st Ohio regiment) had removed our clothes, placed them in kettles, and were boiling them out . . . when a party of rebel cavalry came thundering down upon us. We had no arms with us. Our clothes were in boiling water. The enemy were growing frightfully near. Jumping over the fence, the whole party of us scud through the town for camp like so many wild Indians, as fast as our legs could carry us.
The citizens, supposing we would all be captured, came out in great glee shouting, "Run, Yanks! run, Yanks!" as we fled through the streets. We reached camp in safety, to the great astonishment of our comrades. I asked one old

Appendix

black woman if she didn't blush when she saw us running through the town. She replied, "Why, de Lord God A'mi'ty bress ye, child–I couldn't blush for laughin'." [8]

(At Murfreesboro) a cluster of mangled fellows were huddled about a field hospital. A big brawny trooper, with a bullet in his left leg and another in his right arm, hobbled up holding his wounded arm in his left hand. "Doctor," said he, with much less piety than pain, "the damned rebs came pretty near hitting me." Another fellow, blowing blood copiously from his nose, the point of which had been blown off, interposed, "The damned rascals came damned near missin' me!"[9]

The rebel prisoners were strong admirers of General Jackson, and especially of the great success of his flank movements. "The day after his death," said they, "two angels came down from heaven to carry General Jackson back with them. They searched all through the camp but could not find him. They went to the prayer meeting, to the hospital, and to every other place where they thought themselves likely to find him, but in vain. Finally they were forced to return without him. What was their surprise to find that he had just executed a splendid flank movement, and got into heaven before them!"[10]

One of the soldiers who was in the battle (of Pittsburg Landing) happened to be inordinately fond of card-playing. During the fight he had three of his fingers shot off. Holding up his mangled member, he gazed at it with his eye, "I shall never be able to hold a full hand again!"[11]

A militia captain in North Carolina was marching his company "by the front," when he found himself in front of a gate through which he desired to go. Here was a dilemma. The front of the company was much wider than the opening of the gate, and unless some change should be made in the order of march, part of his men would go full tilt against the fence. Our hero belabored his brain for the proper command, but the words, "By the right flank file left march," obstinately refused to come to his help. He extricated himself from the difficulty in a way which showed his possession of the ready wit of an accomplished guerrilla.

With a bold voice he shouted, "Company, halt- break ranks-march. Form on the other side of the fence!"[12]

A soldier of a Mississippi regiment at Pensacola went to his tent and blankets, the other day, to fight through an ague. A bottle of hot water to his feet not being convenient, some of his comrades went out and picked up one of the numerous shells Colonel Brown sent over during the bombardment, heated it at the fire, and put it to bed with feet. Unhappily, the shell had lost its cap but not exploded. The heat of the camp fire accomplished what Lincoln pyrotechny had failed in, to wit, an explosion. The tent was blown to pieces, and some of the men a little hurt and greatly astonished.[13]

A large and stately brick mansion, which is surrounded by peach orchards, is the property of Mrs. Farrenholt, whose son and husband are in the rebel army. Mrs. Farrenholt is a lady somewhat advanced in years, very secesh in opinion, who has remained on her estate. But she is now dwelling in a small house removed from the danger resulting from guns of her own friends. The other day an officer belonging to the Connecticut artillery corps said, "Madam, good morning. I desire to buy a horse from you."
Lady: "I require what horses I have to plough. I cannot spare one."
Officer (referring to the shells from the enemy): "That will be quite unnecessary. Your people are ploughing up your ground for you."
Lady: "Are they planting also?"
Officer: "They haven't planted any of us yet."
Lady: "Well if they plant any of your blue-coated comrades, I hope they won't sprout!"

LAND WE LOVE:- The South's Last Laugh

The following excerpts derive from General Daniel H. Hill's magazine, *Land We Love* (Charlotte, N.C., 1866-1868), designed to commemorate the South's heroic achievements during the war and sustained by contributions from survivors.

When Johnston's army lay around Smithfield, North

90

Carolina, no flour could be obtained and meal only in such small quantities that two corn-dodgers per man constituted the bread rations. Colonel R—, who had gained such an enviable reputation as the commander of the sharpshooters of Sharps's brigade, was a rigid disciplinarian and determined to stop the practice, so common among the rebel soldiers, of yelling at citizens who passed by, especially if within the conscript age and suspected of keeping out of the army for a mortal antipathy to "vile guns" and "villainous saltpetre."

One day a nice dapper young man, elegantly mounted and handsomely dressed, with a bell-crowned hat, rode by the fun loving regiment and was immediately greeted with the old cry, "Get out of that hat, we know you are thar, see your toes working under it," etc. etc. Colonel R— immediately dashed up crying, "Stop that hallooing. It is coarse and ill mannered. No well bred gentleman would be guilty of it!"

"I don't know, Colonel," replied a Mississippi boy, with a twinkle in his eye, "how you expect men to be well bread on two corn-dodgers a day."[14]

General Jubal A. Early had the famous Louisiana brigade in his division (after the battle of Sharpsburg), and a good many other troops who would not have voted for the Maine liquor law. General Jackson happened to ride in rear of this divisionthat day, and he found the men scattered for miles along the road in every possible attitude, from dancing the polka to sprawling on the ground, some fighting over their battles again, others of a more sentimental turn weeping about the wives and children far away. General Jubal had expended his eloquence and his emphatic Saxon in vain. He had even spread the report that the mountain huts were full of smallpox, but this had only stimulated the curiosity of his prying followers. Conquered at last, he had gone to camp and was toasting his shins that frosty night by a bright fire, when an orderly rode up with a note– "Dispatch from General Jackson, General."

He rose from his seat and fumbled for his spectacles . . . "General Jackson desires to know why he saw so many of your stragglers in rear of your division today?"

"In answer to your note I would state that I think it probable that the reason why General Jackson saw so many of my stragglers on the march today is that he rode in rear of my division. J. A. Early, Major General"[15]

General Early had received a lot of new projectiles and determined to test them. A battery was drawn out,and a group of officers of superior rank to himself – Generals Lee, Longstreet, etc.– posted themselves at right angles to it to observe the firing. The first shot turned over gracefully on its side and went hissing and sputtering close to the mounted men of rank. They modestly retired a few paces. The second shot gave a closer salutation. The captain of the battery now thought it high time to interfere.

Captain: "I think, General, that I had better discontinue the firing. The shells are utterly worthless."

General Early-(eyeing the group of officers): "It looks like there might be promotion in them! You may continue firing, Captain."[16]

No welcome was ever more joyous and hearty than that given by General Jackson to Stuart after his raid around McClellan's rear, a few weeks subsequent to the battle of Sharpsburgh. They both laughed heartily over a picture Stuart had picked up in Pennsylvania, headed, "Where is Stonewall Jackson?" McClellan, with the battles round Richmond fresh in his memory, was represented pointing to his right and saying, "He is there." Halleck was pointing to the left, Pope straight to the front, while Stonewall, as a rough, rugged rebel soldier, had a bayonet within two inches of the rear of the illustrious General whose headquarters were in the saddle.[17]

The 4th North Carolina regiment had waded the north fork of the Shenandoah twice that day in its labor of love in destroying the railroad (at Manassas Gap), and the prospect of a third cold bath was quite alarming to some of the brave boys of that noble regiment. As we passed them at daylight the next morning in the frosty air, we overheard them discussing their probable destination.

"Are they hunting another river for us to wade?"

"No," answered another, "we are on the pike to Winchester, and there is no river between here and there."

"I'll be bound," replied the grumbler, "that they will find another river somewhere."[18]

The pike was firm, but the fields were ankle deep in mud. A boy in a cart, in attempting to pass the 4th North Carolina regiment, was thrown out and seated as gracefully upon the ground as though he had voluntarily taken that position. As he attempted to scramble to his feet, a stalwart soldier marching by him politely remarked, "Keep your seat, my son, I don't want to sit down."[19]

Hugh Mc--, a son of the Emerald Isle, who had volunteered from Fairfield District, South Carolina, in the 6th regiment of infantry, was stationed on the beach of Sullivan's Island with strict orders to walk between two points and to let no one pass him without the countersign, and that to be communicated only in a whisper. Two hours afterward, the corporal, with the relief, discovered by the moonlight Hugh up to his waist in water, the tide having set in since he had been posted.

Hugh: "Who goes there?"

Corporal: "Relief."

Hugh: "Halt, relief. Advance, corporal, and give the countersign."

Corporal: "I am not going in there to be drowned. Come out here and let me relieve you."

Hugh: "Divil a bit of it. The Leftenant tould me not to lave me post."

Corporal: "Well, then, I'll leave you in the water all night (going as he spoke)."

Hugh: "Halt! I'll put a hole in ye if ye pass without the countersign. Them's me orders from the Leftenant (cocking and levelling his gun)."

Corporal: "Confound you, everybody will hear it if I bawl it out to you."

Hugh: "Yes, me darlin', and the Leftenant said it must be given in a whisper. In with yo mo fingor'o on tho trigger and me gun may go off!"

The Corporal had to yield . . . and wade into the faithful sentinel, who remarked that, "The bloody tide has a' most drowned me."[20]

A portly gentleman on the cars between Charleston and Branchville was standing up in all the pride of his magnificent outfit, wholly unconscious that two rebel wags were looking at him with mischief in their eyes. Jim A. and

John B. were never known to spare one of the class to which our fat beau belonged, and a whispered conversation sprang up between them relative to the hero of the rich wardrobe.

Jim A: "The puppy has on a biled shirt as I am a sinner."

John B: "And a white vest!"

Jim A: "Kid gloves and blackened boots!"

John B: "A ring on his fat finger!"

Jim A: "Smells like a baby after drinking catnip tea!"

John A.: "It's cologne the monkey has been putting on his handkerchief."

Jim A: "Can't be as bad as that!"

Jim saunters up to the fat gentleman, assumes manner, an innocent look, and the drawling tones of the pine-wood settlements. "Mister, mout I be so bold as to ax you in what ere battle you got wounded?"

Portly gentleman: "Me? What do you mean, sir?"

John B: "Axin' yer pardon, Jim wants to know whar you gut wounded."

Portly gentleman (sharply): "I have not been wounded at all. What makes you think I have been?"

Jim A. (drawling slowly): "Well, you didn't know but as a bomb mousta bust in yer stomach and kinder swelled you up so."

John B.: "And you smell like the rigimental surgun had been givin' you kloreform or assefedidee to sorter fix you a bit."[21]

December 1864, when Hoke's division was sent out on a reconnaissance upon the Darby Town road, Kirkland's North Carolina brigade was passing us to take position on our left, and greeted us with, "Rice-birds," "Sand-lappers!" etc. One of our men cried out, "Go it, tarheels!" This title the North Carolina troops were justly proud of, it having been given them at the battle of Manassas, where a general remarked, "That regiment of North Carolinians must have tar of their heels to make them stick as they do." To this retort of "Go it, tarheels!" one of Kirkland's men replied, "Yes, we are tarheels, and tar sticks."

"Yes," shouted back another of the South Carolina rice-birds, "when the fire gets hot, the tar runs."[22]

General Doles of Georgia related an instance of

ignorance of tides on the part of a six-footer from the upcountry of Georgia, in his old regiment, the noble 4th Georgia. While posted near Suffolk, he had attempted one morning to cross a little stream when the tide was in. Encumbered with his clothes, the poor fellow had to swim for his life and narrowly escaped from being drowned.

The regiment in the afternoon saw him sit down on the opposite bank of the creek, deliberately take off his shoes and socks, next his clothes, and tie them carefully in a bundle for his back. All these preparations being made, he hesitated before proceeding any further. But at length having made up his mind like a gallant soldier as he was, he plunged boldly into the water, which was nowhere more than two feet deep.[23]

A general officer, who had established a reputation as a good fighter had a morbid desire to be popular with the men. The craving for popularity had made him claim on one occasion the honor of suggesting the issue of hominy ration to the men. And he was by no means neglectful in improving every opportunity for informing them of their indebtedness to him for the favor. The same thirst for applause caused him to wish for a sobriquet, which would the more identify him with the men and endear him to them. So one day he intimated as delicately as might be, his wishes to some privates. These men readily assured him of their willingness to gratify him, but asked for a little delay that they might select a suitable cognomen.

The delay was granted, and a day appointed for the return of the ambitious hero. Punctual to the moment, he was there and thus gracefully introduced the subject: "Jackson is called 'Old Stonewall,' Loring is called 'Old Blizzard,' and Dick Taylor, 'Fighting Dick.' I don't know why it is but some of the boys over there will call me 'Fighting—.'"

The boys not taking the least hint, so delicately given, replied, "We have been thinking of our great obligation to you for that nice ration you got us the other day, and so we have all agreed to call you 'Old Hominy!'"[24]

A distinguished clergyman came to preach to — brigade. Someone made him a present of *real* cheese and crackers, which he was quietly eating by the roadside while the troops were marching past. It was not long before the rebel "sharpshooters" opened fire upon him: "I say, Jim, it's the rale article." "I wonder if the parson's in the blockade-running business." "Mister, I'll whistle Yankee Doodle for you if you'll gin me a smell of that thar Yankee cheese." "I hain't had nothing to eat in three days; please, sir, let me have a slice of that crumb on your whiskers."

When he became conscious that he was the target for all this desultory fire, he began to beat a retreat. Just then a long-legged and gaunt specimen of rebeldom stepped up to him, took off his old slouch hat, made him the most horribly awkward bow and said, "Not any for me, thank you kindly, parson, you are powerful good, but that thar cheese would be too excitin' to my feelins."[25]

A Texian soldier, trudging along one day all alone, met a Methodist circuit rider and at once recognized him as such but affected ignorance of it.

"What army do you belong to?" asked the preacher.

"I belong to the –th Texas regiment, Van Dorn's army," replied the soldier. "What army do you belong to?"

"I belong to the army of the Lord," was the solemn reply.

"Well, then, my friend," said the soldier dryly, "you've got a very long way from Headquarters."[26]

While we camped there, Grant came up to Coffeeville, only twenty miles distant, with a portion of his army. One of our mischievous lads came riding into camp saying that he had just got very important news from the headquarters of General Pemberton. "What is it?" cried out many eager voices.

"There has been a flag of truce in town." "Who sent it?" demanded the excited crowd.

"Old Grant himself," was the reply.

"Well, what does he want?"

"Oh, nothing much– only he says that he wishes to conduct war on civilized principles, and as he intends to shell this town, he requests that the women, children, and the Mississippi regiment of cavalry be removed from all danger."[27]

On the afternoon of the battle of Chancellorsville, the

9th Alabama brought among the prisoners quite a wag. Stopping where the dead lay thickest, he remarked, "You rebs are sharper than you used to be. You used to shoot us anywhere. Now you shoot in the head so as not to bloody our clothes." (He alluded to our practice of stripping the dead of their clothing to cover our nakedness.)[28]

As the soldiers of (Gen. Stephen D.) Lee's corps were wading through the slush after the battle of Bentonville, a citizen rode by on an anatomy of a horse, all covered over with mud, and with tail and mane matted up with burrs and Spanish needles. A soldier accosted the sorry looking rider of the pitiable pony and bantered him for a purchase.

Soldier: "How much will you take for your horse?"
Citizen: "Five hundred dollars."
Soldier: "Agreed! give me the charger."
Citizen: "Where is your money?"
Soldier: "We don't have any of that kind of thing in our army. But I have two years' pay due me, and I'll give that for the war steed.
Citizen: "I'd rather have the money."
Soldier: "And I'd rather have the horse."
Citizen: "You're just joking. They won't let an infantry soldier ride."
Soldier: "Bless your soul! I never thought of riding that thing. I only wanted it to cheer me up."
Citizen: "How could my horse do that?"
Soldier: "Well, I thought of trying to drive him along, so that I might have the comfort of seeing something dirtier, poorer, and meaner than myself!"[29]

After Sherman, with his host of destructives, swept through Georgia, I saw on the roadside a long, lean, lank, lantern-jawed, tallow-faced, dirt eating, transparent, mosquito defying youth, seemingly about twelve years of age and with a voice about as shrill as the treble of a Scotch bagpipe, with great energy and all the strength he was master of, turning nervously the light gray earth with a wooden spade. Soldier-like I did not hesitate to question him, and asked him plainly what he was doing. In his shrill, cracked voice, he fairly screamed, "Can't you see, mister, I'm diggin' a hoel."

"Yes," said I, "my lad, I can– but what are you digging after?"

This time he merely let slip between grunts, "Go-pher."

"Do you think you'll catch him?"

He laid his wooden spade down and turned full upon me his sallow face: "Ketch him, hell– I'm bound to ketch him. We're out o' meat."[30]

(A member of Company F, 14th North Carolina, was giving his friends an account of a very fierce fight on the Peninsula:) We were marching through a thick wood to flank the enemy, and just as we entered the edge of an old field, three or four Yankee batteries opened on us at short range, with grape and cannister. Such a storm I never saw since I was born! The Colonel shouted out, "Lie down!" and down we fell quick, but the dirt and gravel flew all over us, the limbs fell on us, and there was not a thing in the world to shield us from the terrible storm, and we had to just lie still and take it.

"Why didn't you get behind a tree?" suggested a deeply interested listener.

"Tree, hell!" said Company F, "there wasn't trees enough for the officers!"[31]

While A.P. Hill's division was tearing up the Baltimore and Ohio Railroad in the fall of 1862, Lane's brigade was ordered further north than the other brigades – in fact, beyond Hedgesville – where a live rebel was a curiosity. At this time the Quartermaster had not procured new clothing to take the place of the worn, tattered and ragged relics of this campaign into Maryland, and we were a set of ragamuffins– that's a fact. Tearing up railroads is not a very unpleasant business, and we had enjoyed ourselves for about twenty-four hours, when Captain K. of the 7th North Carolina went to a house to get something cooked, and got into quite an interesting conversation with the good lady of the house.

Old Lady: "You is an officer, is you?"

Captain K: "Yes, madam, I am a captain in the 7th North Carolina infantry."

Old Lady (triumphantly): "Thar, now, Betsy Ann, I told you he was an officer. I kin tell an officer whenever I lays my two eyes on 'em. The officers, they has the seats of their breeches patched and the common soldiers, they doesn't."[32]

A private in our company felt the demoralizing influence of war. One day, he gravely remarked, "I'll tell you what, boys, if this war goes on much longer, another Devil will have to be appointed. This old fellow can't attend to all the business that will be on hand."[33]

It was well known throughout the army that Jackson's favorite and first love was the First brigade, better known as the "Stonewall Brigade." It was always put in where the enemy was most stubborn and hardest to break, as broke he was sure to be eventually.

The morning after the battle of Port Republic, when the boys were worn out with hard marching and harder fighting and were resting on their arms, Chaplain — dashed up.

"What news?" cried out many eager voices. "Where are the Yankees?"

"With Old Nick, I hope," piously replied the Chaplain.

"Well, I don't," feelingly replied one of the jaded boys, "for if old Stonewall knew that they were there, he would send the First brigade after them!"[34]

The enemy was reported to be just ahead, and General Jackson rode up to his favorite command with a bright smile upon his face. The boys were in no smiling mood, however. They were hungry and tired, and the proposal of a hard set-to upon empty stomachs was not very cheering. The General saw the gloom and hoped to dispel it by good news. "Well, boys," said he, "I'll let you lead off again. I'm going to give you the post of honor once more."

"Thank you kindly, General," said a hungry fellow. "We have had honor enough. We would rather have a little bread and meat just now!"[35]

At the beginning of the rebellion against Abolition rule, all Confederate Generals of every grade received precisely the same pay, $301 a month. Many were the discussions held and many were the conjectures as to the precise meaning of the odd dollar, when the popular idea was hit by the witticism of a South Carolina soldier: "The $300 are to pay for what the Generals make us do, and the $1 is for what they do themselves!"[36]

At the time the enemy was advancing on Reams' Station, Virginia, there was a deep snow and the roads were almost impassable. The horses of the cavalry were in miserable plight. One man came along on the remains of what had been a pony, with bones protruding and skin hanging loose. The rider wore an enormous pair of Mexican spurs, but 'spite of his vigorous applications, the poor animal stuck in the mud and could not extricate itself. "Halloo," shouted the infantry, "take your horse up on your spurs and shake the mud off him. He'll get along well enough then."[37]

A paroled Federal officer, stopping at one of our hotels, got into a conversation with one of our boys as to the cause of the greater mortality among the Federal than among the Confederate troops. "We are better marksmen," said Jonny Reb, "and fighting the battles of freedom, it was to be expected that we would be more earnest and fire with more coolness and precision."

"Well," drawled Brother Jonathan, " I accounted for it differently. You rebs were so slick with grease and dirt that our balls glanced off without hurting you!"[38]

A cavalryman rode up to our camp one morning, just as we commenced our breakfast, and looking at me for a few moments with a hungry stare said, "Mister, please give me a biscuit. I hain't had a mouthful for three days– today, tomorrow, and next day."

When the –- North Carolina regiment was in Richmond, on its way to take part in the second days fight on the Chickahominy, it bivouacked on the carpet of green in front of the Executive Mansion. Bright and early next morning Governor Letcher was out among the soldiers, and finding the Colonel an old acquaintance, invited him with all his staff officers to walk into his mansion and refresh the inner man in old Virginia style. The invitation was promptly accepted – nobody need doubt that, and as the party marched up the stone steps of the house, unknown to the Colonel, a tall, rawboned and very dirty private followed closely on his heels. A soldier who was looking on from the park shouted out, "I say, Kreps, where in the mischief are you agoin'?"

"Goin'?" shouted Kreps unabated and with a mental swagger, "Why, I promised to follow our gallant Kurnel to death or victory, and I am agwine to do it!"[39]

Captain Davy Crockett of Arkansas, grandson of the celebrated Crockett of Tennessee and Texas, was going home on a leave of absence accompanied by a soldier during the last days. He had ridden all day, and hungry and weary, he stopped at nightfall at a house by the wayside and asked for lodging.

"Can't take you," said an old man at the door. "Got nothing to eat. The rebels, they comes along and eats up all we got, and then the Yankees, they comes along and they eats up the balance!"[40]

In July 1864, a portion of Carter's batallion of artillery, Army of Northern Virginia, was stationed below Richmond. Private John T. Mills retired under fire by about fifty marines. Looking over my shoulder, I saw him stop, coolly inspect his pursuers and then start at a run again. When I had reached a place where I could talk with him without danger of unreasonable interruption from our Northern brethren, I waited till he came up and inquired, "Mills, what on earth did you stop for– right in the hottest of the firing?" "Well," replied he, "I wanted to gauge my running, and I stopped to see whether it was a cavalry or infantry after me. I was running on the infantry schedule, but if it had been cavalry behind me, I would have run on the cavalry schedule and gone a little faster."[41]

I got my first bad wound in '62, and as my home was in Yankee hands, I was furloughed to go where I pleased, and I went to Alabama. I took up my abode with an old lady who was a fire-eating hater of Yankees, and has as little toleration for a bluecoat as for the Queen's English. One day, when the conversation turned rather gloomily upon the prospect of the final success of the Yankees, she flew into a great passion and cried out, "Never, never– they may captivate all the men, they may arrogate all the women, they may fisticate all the land, but they can never congregate the South, never, never, never!"[42]

(Three days after the Yankees took Jackson, Mississippi) and set their faces towards Vicksburg, my brother-in-law went out to look and see what was left to him. Not a vestige of anything movable remained. His wife's and children's clothes were gone or torn into ribbons, the house was stripped, the provisions gone, except half a barrel of sugar, which was polluted by them. An old negro man, who remained faithful, reported they had several times set fire to the house, which he extinguished. They had washed their feet over the cisterns, letting the water run into them, and killed every living thing except one hen, which had escaped by hiding in the grass, and about fifteen chickens of from a week or two to a few days old, which were the remains of a hundred and fifty of the same ages. These were all trying to follow the old hen who, under the circumstances, must have had a Yankee cross in her, as she was pecking at them while they were shying around with a truly orphan air. As he looked around upon the desolation, I asked him what he thought of the Yankees now.

He gave a glance around and said, "I don't believe there is a man living damned enough liar to tell the truth about them!"[43]

Four or five members of Company H, 5th Mississippi, while lying in the trenches around Atlanta in 1864 had a brief respite from the annoying shot and shell. We had got a large lot of biscuit and expected to have a fine time of it in enjoying the unusual banquet. But "human hopes oft deceive us." While we were sitting like Turks on a blanket, pitching into the biscuit and old Tommie R--, a long, lean specimen of rebeldom, was stretching out his bony arm for the biggest one in the pile, a minnie took off a piece of his hand as big as a five dollar Confederate note and pitched him over upon our stock of biscuits. George H-- jerked at him and cried out, "Damn it, boys, don't let the old man bleed on the biscuits!"[44]

In (January '65) I visited Staunton, the headquarters of old Jubal [Early] and the remnant of the gallant little army of the Valley. The day after my arrival, being a bright Sunday morning, General Early surprised his staff by announcing his intention of going to church, requesting their company. . . .

The sermon was a good one, earnest and impressive:

102

"Suppose, my Christian friends, that those who have laid for centuries in their graves should arise now and come forth from their quiet resting places; and marching in their white shrouds should pass before this congregation, by thousands and tens of thousands, what would be the result?"

"Ah!" exclaimed old Jubal in a stage whisper, "I'd conscript every damn one of them."[45]

On the James River, near -- Bluff, old Mr. Tugmuddle, with his numerous daughters, lived within a short distance of the river bank and very close to our camp–near where, in summer, the soldiers were wont to bathe. So near, indeed, that one day "Colonel Cramp" received a visit from Mr. Tugmuddle in which Tugmuddle took occasion to say, "Sir, your soldiers strip and bathe, sir, right before the eyes of my daughters, who are modest young ladies to whom the sight that they are daily made to witness is extremely offensive."

The Colonel, with gallantry, resolved and promised that the evil complained of should be remedied, and he stationed a guard thereafter on the bank to make the soldiers go further up the stream. But a few days elapsed when old Tug made the same complaint again. That evening at dress parade, orders, stricter than ever, were promulgated forbidding our boys to bathe nearer to old Tug's house than a certain point about five hundred yards distant therefrom. Within a few days, however, Tug came back with his old complaint.

"Why," said the Colonel, "have my orders been disobeyed? Surely your daughters can't see my men now – five hundred yards off!"

"Yes, sir, they can."

"What! see men bathing over five hundred yards off!"

"But, sir," said old Tug, "my gals have spy glasses!"[46]

Notes

[1] Frank Moore, *Anecdotes, Poetry and Incidents of the War* (New York: Scribner's Brothers, 1866), 123.

[2] *Ibid.*, 144-45.

[3] *Ibid.*, 179.

[4] *Ibid.*, 187.

[5] *Ibid.*, 214.

[6] *Ibid.,* 248.
[7] *Ibid.,* 253.
[8] *Ibid.,* 302-3.
[9] *Ibid.,* 305.
[10] *Ibid.,* 357.
[11] *Ibid.,* 358.
[12] *Ibid.,* 359.
[13] *Ibid.,* 465.
[14] *Ibid.,* May, 1866, 68.
[15] *Ibid.,* 71.
[16] *Ibid.,* 72.
[17] *Ibid.,* 75.
[18] *Ibid.,* August, 288.
[19] *Ibid.*
[20] *Ibid.,* 292.
[21] *Ibid.*
[22] *Ibid.,* 293.
[23] *Ibid.,* 294.
[24] *Ibid.,* September, 1866, 345.
[25] *Ibid.,* October, 1866, 431-32.
[26] *Ibid.,* November, 1866, 103.
[27] *Ibid.,* January, 1867, 215.
[28] *Ibid.,* 216.
[29] *Ibid.,* February, 1867, 297-98.
[30] *Ibid.,* 300.
[31] *Ibid.,* November, 1867, 83-84.
[32] *Ibid.,* February, 1868, 345-46.
[33] *Ibid.,* March, 1868, 440.
[34] *Ibid.,* 433.
[35] *Ibid.,* 435.
[36] *Ibid.,* 433.
[37] *Ibid.,* 439.
[38] *Ibid.,* 441.
[39] *Ibid.,* April, 1868,532.
[40] *Ibid.,* June, 1868, 178.
[41] *Ibid.,* 180-181.
[42] *Ibid.,* 183.
[43] *Ibid.,* July, 1868, 279.
[44] *Ibid.,* August, 1868, 359.
[45] *Ibid.,* September, 1868, 441.
[46] *Ibid.,* October, 1868, 531.

Appendix